THE
BEREAVED
PARENT

D0293729

HUMAN HORIZONS SERIES

THE BEREAVED PARENT

HARRIET SARNOFF SCHIFF

A CONDOR BOOK
SOUVENIR PRESS (E&A) LTD

Copyright © 1977 by Harriet Sarnoff Schiff

First published in the U.S.A. by
Crown Publishers Inc., New York

First British Edition published 1979 by
Souvenir Press (Educational & Academic) Ltd. 43 Great Russell Street
London WC1B 3PA
Reissued 1992
Reprinted 1999, 2008

All Rights Reserved. No part of this publication
may be reproduced, stored in a retrieval system,
or transmitted, in any form or by any means, electronic,
mechanical, photocopying, recording or otherwise, without
the prior permission of the Copyright owner

ISBN 978 0 285 64891 3

Printed in Great Britain by
MPG Books Ltd, Bodmin, Cornwall

ACKNOWLEDGMENTS

There are many people who make up the framework of my professional and private life who had a part in helping with this work. There is Lucille DeView who hired me for my first reporting job and who has been my friend and editor through the years.

There are dear friends who helped us when their help was needed particularly. People like the Stones and Ambroses, who seem never to have left our side.

There are dear and close family—our parents, sisters, and brothers—who agonized with us stage by stage while feeling their own loss at our son's death.

There are our children, Dale and Stacie, and Cindy our daughter-in-law, who ran interference while this book was being written. At the same time, they offered their unstinting support when it was needed.

There are the people at Crown Publishers, Inc. who recognized the need for this book.

Also for their contributions and insights I wish to thank Ronald Koenig, founder of the Center for Death, Dying, and Lethal Behavior at University of Detroit; Dr. Bruce Danto, psychiatrist, author, and founder of the Detroit Suicide Prevention and Drug Information Center of Michigan; Dr. Joseph Fischoff, Chief of Psychiatry, Children's Hospital of Michigan; Dr. Elliot Luby, Director of the Outpatient Department of Detroit's Lafayette Clinic; Dr. F. Paul Pearsall, Chief of the Problems of Daily Living Clinic at Sinai Hospital of Detroit.

A special thank-you to Dr. Edward Green, Chief of Cardiology, Children's Hospital of Michigan, for his guidance and the kindness he showed while our son was alive.

I especially wish to thank my friend and often mentor Dr. John J. Pollack, Chief of Staff of Children's Hospital of Michigan for his support, guidance, and friendship during Robby's lifetime and after his death.

Also, I wish to extend my appreciation to the countless fellow bereaved parents who allowed me to prod their memories and probe their grieving to enable me to write this book.

Most of all, there is Sandy, a special husband and friend, who suffered with me and cried with me and laughed with me and who helped so affirmatively with the dissection of emotions necessary to comprehend the stages of our grieving.

Thank you.

CONTENTS

To the memory of our own little boy blue,

Robby

INTRODUCTION

There is a tale about a prince fleeing from revolutionaries determined to kill him and take away his throne. The prince, terrified, sought shelter in a peasant's cottage.

Although the peasant had no idea the frightened man was a member of the nobility he gave the prince refuge by telling him to hide under the bed. The prince had no sooner done so when his pursuers battered down the door and began to search the cottage.

The revolutionaries searched everywhere. When they came to the bed they decided to prod it with knives rather than move the cumbersome piece of furniture. At last they left.

The prince, pale but alive, crawled from under the bed after hearing the pursuers depart. He turned to the peasant then and said, "I think you should understand that you have just saved the life of your prince. Name three favours and I will grant them.''

The peasant, a simple man, thought for a while and said:

"My cottage is in great disrepair and I have not had the money to fix it. Can this be done?''

"Fool!" cried the prince. "Of all things in the world, why did you ask so small a favour? I will honour your wish, but what is your next request?''

"Sire, my neighbour sells the same wares as me in the market-place. Would it be possible to change his location so both of us could make a better livelihood?''

"Idiot," said the prince. "Of course I will do as you wish. What foolishness, when you could have riches, to ask such nonsense! Take care that you do not anger me with another silly request.''

No longer able to restrain his curiosity, the peasant said, "As my third request I ask only that you tell me how you felt as the knives were being pushed through the bed.''

The prince, infuriated, shouted, "How dare you offend majesty by asking of my emotions? For this act I will have you beheaded tomorrow!''

The prince called in a few of his retainers and had the hapless man carried off to the local jail.

All through the night the man wept for his folly and feared what would happen on the morrow.

When the sun rose his jailors came to him and led him into a courtyard where an executioner with his black hood stood awaiting the terrified man.

Forced to kneel on the block he heard a soldier call "One, two . . ." but before he could say three, another soldier on horseback came tearing into the courtyard calling "Stop! The prince commands it.''

With those words the executioner, whose blade had been

resting on the peasant's neck, withdrew the sword. The shaking man arose and faced the soldier who had saved his life.

"His Highness gives you his pardon and orders me to give you this note," said the soldier.

The peasant, relieved to the point of tears, began to read the few terse words:

"As your final favour you wanted to know how I felt under that bed when the revolutionaries came. I have granted your request because now you know!"

The prince had shown the peasant more graphically than words could possibly have done just what the horrendous ordeal had been like.

The prince, no fool, had realized that some things are beyond describing. No matter how eloquent the words, their impact can fall flat when not accompanied by a similar experience.

And so it is with bereaved parents.

No one has gone through this catastrophe without thinking sometime or other, "You can't possibly know what it feels like!"

It is rare not to think this as loving friends and family vainly try to comfort and soothe. All their kindness is almost meaningless in the face of the despair a parent feels when outliving a child.

As the prince illustrated to the peasant, the emotions one feels are only believable and truly understood by a fellow bereaved parent.

When our son, aged ten, died in 1968, we were surrounded by well-meaning, well-intentioned people who would try to ease our grief and diminish our pain with assurances that things would be better. They failed. My husband and I would look at them, all of them, and think, "What do they know!" After all, they would leave our house of mourning and go home to their intact families.

What we needed then was somebody who could say, "I survived the same ordeal you are now enduring. You can do it. I have some suggestions that might help."

We would have placed a value beyond price on such assurances. We could have avoided some dreadful pitfalls had we been warned by people who had undergone the same grief we now faced.

Not long ago, a young man aged eighteen, a casual friend of our surviving son, died. Although we did not know his parents intimately, we knew them well enough to make a condolence call. They had a house full of people. Yet when they saw us they left everyone and asked us to sit with them in another room. The father put his head on my husband's shoulder and cried. My husband held the newly bereaved man in his arms and patted him and quieted him. The mother grasped my hands and cried.

We did not possess some secret knowledge that gave us special comforting skills. What we had was something few could give them. We had experience. When they saw us, they saw a mother and father with a dead child who were able to cope.

We sat with the couple for nearly an hour and assured them they would survive. We cautioned them to avoid a number of mistakes we had made. They listened.

Nearly a year later, I ran into the mother. She thanked me for making that condolence visit and told me that although others had offered advice that made sense, it went in one ear and out the other. What we told them they remembered and understood because our advice came after undergoing what they had undergone.

Recentiy, two women who had known each other from high school days met and stopped to chat briefly in my presence. When one of them departed, the other turned to me and said, "There goes the kindest and best person I have ever known.

"I had not seen her for ten years when my daughter died. Yet she called me when she read about it in the newspaper. She said she hoped she wasn't intruding but her own boy had died a year previously. All she really wanted to say besides being sorry was that we would survive. We would make it."

The woman wiped tears from her eyes and added, "I know many people came to us when it happened, but of everyone, I remember what that lady did. She offered me reassurance when I had none."

If I can do that for you, if I can indeed convince you that your life can still have meaning, then forcing painful recollections to the surface in order to write this book was well worth the effort.

I recently spoke to a group of bereaved parents. As happens with all guest speakers, some of my listeners came up afterward to thank me. One man shook my hand and said my vitality was encouraging. Another parent, the mother of a murdered boy, said that, despite attending monthly meetings at which professional counselling people talked about different aspects of grieving, this was the first time she ever left a session where someone had extended hope.

I am certain that, somewhere along the line, these advisors had told them that eventually they would begin to live again, but somehow the message did not register. Obviously mine did, because what I had to say came not from schooling but from suffering.

Certainly, in the early days after our son died, no one could have patted us on our heads and convinced us everything would be all right. Nor will this book do that for you. It will, with the help of parents who have successfully coped and professional people who work with bereavement, offer guidelines and practical step-by-step suggestions to aid you.

We bereaved parents come in all ages. We are not limited to

any specific colour or faith. Parents with dead babies, parents whose sons died in war, parents who are elderly and lived to bury their middle-aged children, all have a great need to know that others have experienced the emotions they are feeling and that these others are dealing effectively with both their bereavement and life.

But just as important as knowing you are not alone is knowing you can and must learn to carry on despite this most unnatural of disasters.

The death of a child is frequently called the ultimate tragedy. I believe this is true. But it is a tragedy that must not be compounded by allowing everything around you to die also. There are other children, mates, sisters, brothers, friends, who need and deserve to see you functioning well.

This book is intended to help you regain that level.

You can't prevent birds of sorrow flying over your head—but you can prevent them from building nests in your hair.

—CHINESE PROVERB

BEREAVEMENT

The man, seeing his son near death, changed from his rich robes to sackcloth and from his diet of plenty to fasting, hoping his sacrifices would help the boy he dearly loved. When, seven days later, the youngster died despite the finest medical attention of his day, the man once again put on his luxurious garments and sat down to an abundant feast. When friends asked him how he could eat with his child newly dead, he replied he had done all that was humanly possible while the boy was alive and now that he was gone, it was time to pick up the pieces of living and go on with life.

The man was King David.

The wise king had come to a truth that countless parents in their pain have also found.

The living must go on with life.

Unless we are suicidal, we have no alternative.

But how we continue our lives and how we come to terms with this, the ultimate tragedy, is crucial.

Whether a son or daughter died in a muddy rice paddy in Southeast Asia or in an antiseptic hospital ward, in a sudden accident or after prolonged illness, the result is the same.

You, the child's mother or father, seem to have violated a natural law. You have outlived your child. Tragically, at the same time, a period when you are most confused, you have to make a fundamental determination.

From here on, will you have a life or an existence?

When I was faced with the decision, I opted for life.

Although there were many months when I didn't really care, when I was actually frightened by the idea of living forty or fifty years after my young son had died, I know my decision was right.

It is painful, even now, years later, to recall him lying in the intensive care unit at the University of Alabama hospital, wired to electronic gadgets like some Rube Goldberg infernal machine, desperately fighting to survive his open heart surgery.

It is horrendous to think of the moment when a doctor asked my husband to come into a little conference room inside the unit.

We knew by the feverish activity surrounding our son's bed that something had gone terribly wrong. Although he had survived the massive surgery for twenty-four hours, suddenly he appeared to be in a crisis. Doctors, including one who became a dear friend, were running and somehow had difficulty looking us in the eye.

All that time, and it seemed like hours, we stood there helpless; unable to do what parents instinctively seek to do—succour their child and protect it and keep it from harm. We were not even allowed in the room. We were not even allowed to touch him or speak to him.

I remember my heart hammering and thinking it would actually explode as I stood there holding my husband's hand, looking for someone to say it would be all right even though I knew it wouldn't be.

When the doctor asked my husband to come into the small conference room at the side of the unit, I asked if I couldn't accompany them. He looked at me solemnly and said I certainly could.

We followed him, and on that bright sunny March morning we were told Robby had died.

I screamed. A nurse, tears suddenly coming to her eyes, offered me a tranquillizer and I thought, how inane. Robby was dead and I was being given a pill to make it go away. Impossible.

But from that distant time—with memories I can never hope to erase and, indeed, some that I would not wish to eradicate—I have learned that life does go on and that is only as it should be. The problem we bereaved parents face is that life is going on around us while we frequently think we have become incapable of going on with life.

More important, I have learned through trying—sometimes failing, sometimes succeeding—that there are certain steps a bereaved parent can and must take in order to retain any meaning to that life. Any quality.

At the outset, it will not be easy. All too often, it is a matter of fighting the natural tide of your grief as well as your very natural desire to give in to that grief. Time must be allowed for both. It is just as unnatural to walk around with a frozen grin after such a tragedy as it is never to stop weeping. It is a matter of highly personalized balance.

Unfortunately, this is not the sort of balance that can be

weighed or measured or seen. There is no formula for what is enough of either. It is, instead, something that is felt. Like a blind person confronted suddenly with new surroundings, your balance of laughing and crying is something you and you alone must grope toward.

For some, that balance of laughing and crying could be the easing of grief for an hour a day while for others it could be allowing a fit of weeping for that period.

What is important is that there be both.

Bereaved parents come in all ages. It does not appear to make a difference whether one's child is three, thirteen, or thirty if he dies. The emotion in each of us is the same.

How could it be that a parent outlives a child?

One woman in her eighties still deeply grieves over the loss of her forty-five-year-old daughter. Although she is a great-grandmother and had nearly half a century of love from her daughter, she says nothing can ever be right for her again.

"Joanie called me every day. I never interfered with her life and she never interfered in mine. But she was such a big part of my world, and now she is gone."

The woman frequently bemoans being left alive to cope with all that grief.

Equally sad are the young parents of babies who have suffered crib death. They are the ones who kiss their apparently healthy children good night, put them to bed, and find them the next morning, dead with no warning.

Death is no respecter of wealth or colour.

It does not matter whether the child comes of a monied family or a poor one. Certainly no expense was spared in our efforts to save Robby and it ended just as if we were destitute. He was dead.

A black mother, subsisting on meagre finances, who cared

for and fed her child just as I did mine, felt the same sense of loss I did when her twenty-two-year-old son was shot by an unknown assailant. He was dead and she was alive.

A medical secretary whose only child was killed during the Vietnam conflict felt the same emotion. She had cared. She had loved. Her son was dead.

The backgrounds vary, but the emotion is universal. Children have died. What an unutterable waste!

Although I still feel a sense of loss—and frustration at the unused years my ten-year-old son should have had—I have learned to survive despite a stunting heartache. Most of all, I have learned to enjoy life despite feeling a lament behind my laughter.

When a child dies, it is inevitable that there is not a clean break. Along with the funeral and horror, there is a great deal of emotional wreckage left as a residue of the tragedy.

Cruelly enough, in the vast majority of cases, not only do we parents have to endure the grief of having a dead child, more often than not we also undergo severe family crises. Drunkenness, separation, divorce, alienation, are frequently the aftermath of losing a daughter or son.

In addition, a bereaved couple all too often is jolted by a further loss—the loss of illusion about each other.

Shortly after Robby died, an older couple came to offer condolences. Although they were grandparents, they obviously found it difficult to utter the right words of comfort despite every best intention.

Finally, after an awkward half hour the wife said, "At least you have each other for comfort."

It would seem on the surface that this would be true. After all, both my husband and I had been in the same hospital room, had suffered the same loss, and together had seen our precious child buried.

Certainly having each other for comfort would be the logical solution. Unfortunately, as a number of parents whose child died have discovered, it is impossible to give comfort when you feel an equal grief.

Parents in all walks of life, many now divorced, agreed on the major problem. Too much was expected of the mate and too little was received.

The depth of this phase of the tragedy did not become apparent in the early days after Robby died. My husband and I were too busy trying to put the pieces back together and too busy receiving callers to realize that we could not comfort each other.

Visualize two people pulling a cart for many miles. When one grows tired, he eases his grip, thereby letting a larger share of the burden fall on the other. The one left pulling grows resentful of the increased burden and voices anger. The first is now resentful because his exhaustion has not been treated sympathetically.

When the positions reverse, the resentment reverses.

I saw an example of this seesawing of sympathy in a couple I had considered well mated. Their son, a young man about to be married, was murdered in a back alley.

The father, a factory worker, who has held the same job for over twenty years and once took pride in a good attendance record, now immerses his grief in drinking bouts and misses days of work at a time. Instead of going to his job he takes his bottle of whisky, goes to his bedroom and drinks and drinks and drinks.

His wife feels revulsion rather than sympathy. She has threatened to leave him if he doesn't stop drinking. To no avail. She said she is powerless to help him and is furious because he is not helping her.

"Each of us has his own misery. I can't help his. He can't

help mine. That's not how it's supposed to be, I guess. But that is how it really is," says his wife.

Seeing things as they really are is very painful when a child dies. Ruthless fact is the last thing we want. Somewhere in the back of our minds, especially at first, is the idea that this is all a dream. He couldn't really be dead. She just could not be gone. We will wake up and it will only have been a dream.

But gradually most of us reach the point where we must acknowledge that our son or daughter is truly gone. That is the time when a bereaved parent is faced with life's harshest reality.

Ultimately, though, facing that reality is what we need in order to go on with life when a child is dead. Facing it could well begin with something as simple as language. Robby did not "pass on." Nor did he "fly to heaven" or "go to his just reward."

He died.

Those two words are cold, brutal, and true.

During the time before I decided to live and not exist, I used such euphemisms in even my innermost thoughts. It was only when I could think "Robby is dead" that I could also think "but I am alive."

The function of friends is to be the sounding board for grief.

—JOSHUA LOTH LIEBMAN

BEREAVEMENT AND THE FUNERAL

Once, a Chinese servant asked his employer, an Occidental, for permission to attend the funeral of a cousin.

The man magnanimously granted permission, but asked in a scathing voice whether the ancient Chinese custom of leaving a bowl of rice at the graveside would be followed.

"Certainly," the servant replied.

Laughing, the employer asked when the cousin would eat the rice.

"Oh," said the servant, "about the same time that your aunt who died last week smells the flowers you placed on her grave!"

In other words, to each his own.

Although burial customs vary according to beliefs and religion and country, the imperative thing about a funeral is that it not become a further source of pain to already grieving parents.

Very important to remember for most parents is that when their child is lying there dead, there can be no really "nice" funeral. In most cases, all but the most religious have not yet been reconciled to their grief. The funeral then becomes a matter of getting over the most treacherous ground. Frequently, parents of dead children make mistakes at this time that years later seem ridiculous. These are the things we wish could be undone. Realistically, they cannot. The greatest comfort we can derive is to know these mistakes were made out of poor judgment at a time when our senses were outraged.

Although there are people nowadays who do not believe in the standard funeral, who believe instead in a memorial service sometime after a person dies, I found the traditional service with its set and ancient guidelines easier to cope with than decision-making in a new direction would have been.

When Robby died, we were in a state of numbness which almost always is the initial reaction to bereavement. Because we were unable really to concentrate, having rigid religious burial rules made things a great deal simpler.

It took as much as we could handle to make minimal decisions like what clothes our son would wear and what price we wished to pay for his burial.

The only small break with traditional burial custom was our insistence that Robby not be eulogized by a cleric who had only met him once or twice. We ourselves knew well what our son was and what we had lost. We asked instead that the service contain only some biblical parallel, and we left its selection up to the rabbi.

He made an excellent choice. He told the story of David and how he did everything possible for his son while the boy was alive, but, when the son died, David once again took up the business of living.

It was a selection that served a twofold purpose: first, we did not wish to be subjected to a heartrending reminder of what Robby was and could never be again; second, it suggested a path to follow after the funeral—to attempt to emulate David and to take up life once again.

In general, though, the rabbi's words, well chosen as they were, did little to comfort us. We were, we felt, beyond comforting.

Unlike ourselves, there are people who become intensely involved in planning their child's funeral. One woman, a devout Catholic whose eight-year-old daughter died in an automobile accident, selected every psalm, prayer card, and hymn for her daughter's funeral.

"I felt this was the final earthly thing I could do for my daughter's remains. Certainly, I cried for myself while planning her funeral, but I knew she had gone back to God and for her I was happy."

Although many people opt for traditional funerals, there are those who believe the only meaningful burial has to be completely personalized.

One woman, an American Indian whose son drowned, thought the finest tribute she could pay her fourteen-year-old was to bury him in the traditional Indian finery he used while engaged in his hobby of tribal dancing. According to her wishes, the youngster wore his loin breech and a beaded shirt. Following the traditional Catholic service, a member of the boy's Indian tribe spoke to mourners and told them the lad was now with Manitou, the Great Spirit, and would watch over the grieving family. Through it all, the mother said she felt a satisfaction in having arranged something that would please her dead son.

Another family had their daughter's remains cremated after a brief visitation period. Thirty days later, they held a twilight garden memorial service for her where friends and family got up and spoke about the dead girl or read biblical passages. One observer who attended the rite said it was the only appropriate one for this particular family.

One Protestant minister, faced with parents of two different faiths, read passages from the play *Our Town*, attempting to minimize offence to the dead child's Catholic father.

I repeat, to each his own. There is no right or wrong type of funeral service.

As more is learned about handling bereavement, however, most psychiatric personnel who help grieving families have come to view the private funeral service with disfavour. They generally frown upon this practice because of their emphasis on the need for support during all phases following the death of a child.

Most often, the private funeral seems to be the wish of parents whose child committed suicide or was involved in criminal activity. Such parents often feel shame compounded with their grief.

Yet, it would appear to me that *they*—almost more than other bereaved parents—need every bit of loving and caring and kindness that can be offered by friends and acquaintances.

What could be more tragic than to have a child dead by his or her own hand? Or how sad to have reared a child who died a criminal!

To voluntarily remove oneself from caring people by holding the private funeral seems only to heighten a pain that is nearly unbearable.

The private service brings another great disservice to mourners. People generally feel that, if the funeral is private, so may be the grieving afterward. Not only will they tend to stay away out of fear of intruding but it seems also true that if they do come they will avoid at all costs discussing the tragedy.

Therefore, by holding a private funeral, very often the support system particularly necessary to parents in this situation may be denied them.

I cannot honestly remember who was at the funeral or the cemetery when Robby died, but I have an overall recollection of being surrounded—almost cushioned—by people. Now, there are times when I go through the messages of condolence and the chapel visitors' book signed by those who attended the funeral, and I am still grateful for whatever time people gave us out of their lives. It was not easy for them but it did an immeasurable amount of good for us.

Moreover, though there is a great reluctance on the part of many people in the immediate family, psychiatrists maintain it is very important for survivors to view the dead body of a loved one. They say it is wrong to follow that old bromide of "I want to remember him as he was." They claim this reason for not viewing the body is a form of death denial because "as he was" was alive. But he is no longer alive.

People are often profoundly reluctant to attend the funeral of a child. They experience a great fear of inadequacy, of not being able to say or do the right thing. But their presence at this time can be most supportive.

Richard Obershaw, a faculty member of the University of Minnesota School of Mortuary Science, when speaking at a seminar for social workers, confirmed the importance to the bereaved family of people attending a funeral. He said that not only do people need comfort at this time, they crave it badly enough to advertise for it!

People, he said, pay an additional sum of money to the funeral director in order to have a notice inserted in local newspapers. They are saying, in effect, I need your help and here is where I will be at a given time and place to receive whatever consolation you are able to give.

Many funeral directors as well as psychologists who have

contact with people at times of grief say viewing the body is an integral part of the healing process that must follow a death. They maintain doing so lessens the length of time for the denying of death because people will not reject ultimately something they have seen with their own eyes.

At Robby's funeral, my husband and I went to view the body. I gazed at my dead son for a second and literally ran from the sight of his stillness.

One father, upon seeing his dead son who was killed while on duty in Vietnam, threw himself onto the open casket and screamed until the funeral director finally led him to a chair.

Yes, the sight is painful . . . but much in the same way as cauterizing a wound is painful. Just as healing may not begin without that very painful procedure, psychiatrists believe the same principle applies to viewing the body.

In the healing years since Robby died, I have reviewed what we did correctly and, as well, the areas in which we erred. Because of my protective instinct as a mother, I made a massive error in judgment at the funeral. I would not allow my son, aged twelve, to view the body of his dead brother because of the horror *I* felt seeing it. Difficult though it would have been, he should not have been denied this right. Unfortunately, no one told me I would harm my son with my protectiveness. And harm him it did because it took many years for him to lay his brother's ghost to rest.

My daughter, then four, did not attend the funeral and therefore had even less grasp of her brother's death. She is resentful even after all these years that she was cheated of the experience.

It has taken some years for me to resolve my sorrow at having made such mistakes. I know now that I am not alone. Many of us upon looking back at how we handled decisions at the funeral would now make changes.

But I have put my wrong decisions where I feel they belong. They rest now in the category of mistakes that cannot be undone and are therefore best forgotten. That part of my life is over.

As difficult as viewing the body can be, a very good case can be made for the argument that parents of soldiers listed as missing suffer almost more than parents of dead soldiers. People believe what they see, and laying someone to rest can be impossible when there is no body to lay to rest. Many such parents believe deep in their hearts that they will see their children again. Maybe just around the next corner . . .

How can parents grieve and then rebuild a life when that grief is interspersed with hope that, somewhere, their child will reappear?

It is not only the parents of soldiers who are afflicted with this nightmarish problem.

One father who suffered through both stages, the missing and the certainty, has his own conclusion. His son, a boy of nine, drowned while swimming in a lake. The father searched and searched and continued to look for the body of his son for more than a month until it was found by a fisherman.

"His body was ugly and distorted," said the father, "but when I saw it, finally, I knew he was dead. The pain was unbearable when I wasn't searching before that. Once his body was found I was almost relieved. It was like a thousand pounds off my shoulders."

This father's intensity of feeling obviously is the rule rather than the exception because newspapers frequently carry stories of rewards and pleas of grieving families for the return of their children's bodies when the youngsters had met with the kinds of death where the bodies are not easily retrieved. Parents of soldiers missing in action are an example of this sort of searching.

Somehow, without this visible and irrefutable sign of death, there is something unfinished about the state of grieving undergone by a parent, something that heightens the sense of disbelief we already feel in those first terrible days.

Also, during these first days there is an additional and important purpose to the funeral in that it gives the bereaved family a socially acceptable setting in which to grieve. And the importance of that grieving process cannot be overstated. One funeral director, who holds a master's degree in social work, recently went so far as to say that Jacqueline Kennedy Onassis, with her magnificent public stoicism at the funeral of the assassinated president, "set grieving back a hundred years. She created an example of dignity for the world that people emulated just as they emulated her dress and little dinner parties. The only harm in emulating this brave woman arose when people did not stop to think that in private she cried and probably screamed just as we all do."

"Mrs. Onassis," said the funeral director, "set a tone for grieving that people began to follow blindly—and one that became expected by onlookers. Some of my clients, bereaved parents, actually were ashamed of their own comparative 'lack of control' as this attitude filtered down to the general population. I question what kind of control should have to be maintained by the parent of a dead child at such a catastrophic time."

The question he raised is valid because too much control can be as dangerous as too little. Of course, as in all things there must be limitations. While total "stiff upper lipism" is unnatural, so, I have discovered, is an ongoing lack of self-discipline.

My husband, whom I consider a victim of the masculine-must-be-strong ethic, showed almost no outward signs of the horror he felt. Instead he served as the comforter at the funeral. The moral supporter. Several years after Robby's death, his agony was still so great that he needed psychiatric help, and in the privacy of his doctor's office he cried. And only then did he begin to heal.

I, being a female and the Bereaved Mother, was given most of the support including loving shoulders upon which to cry. I availed myself of them often and at length.

Sometimes when the unthinkable is thought about in advance, good can result. This became the case with where our son is buried. While not all people can be fortunate enough to have such a place available to them, we believe it has helped us through the grieving procedure.

One Sunday, some months before Robby was scheduled for surgery, my husband and I took a drive and quite by chance saw a beautiful parklike cemetery with well-tended grounds and no raised markers. We discussed then that, if Robby did not survive his operation, this was where we would bury him. Somehow that particular cemetery offers serenity to me.

We decided on this place with its parklike setting not so much for Robby as for our other children. Just as we believe the funeral is for the living in memory of the dead, we felt the cemetery should serve the same function. We wanted our children to have a place to visit their brother's grave that would not frighten them. We were proven right the first time our daughter asked to go there. Whatever she projected from ghostly television programs just could not be reinforced when viewing this garden setting.

There are many parents who would object to this place. It is new and in its newness it lacks the beauty of tradition and also perhaps, for some, the reminder that there is continuity in death as well as in life.

Also, not all parents, whether for religious or financial reasons, have such choices. Many children are buried as lovingly and with as much respect and dignity in traditional cemeteries.

There is truly no right or wrong. Instead, it is a question of doing what best we can with the funds and mental facilities we have available at the time.

Sometimes unique situations arise and adjustments are necessary. The mobility of the modern family can become a factor in making burial arrangements. One family, whose husband's job requires moving every few years, decided to bury their daughter in New Jersey, which they considered home base even though they lived more than five hundred miles away.

"She is buried next to her grandparents in our old hometown. We are so rootless that we believed this would be best for all of us and for her," said the girl's mother.

Although I felt my thinking process was numbed when Robby died, I was lucky enough to have regained it by the time we were ready to take our daughter to the cemetery. Sometimes it takes years before a parent is healed enough to handle situations properly. What worked for us may not have worked for everyone.

Along with the parklike atmosphere, we took an additional precaution before taking our daughter to the cemetery. We called ahead, explained we were bringing our young child and asked that they not water the grass at his grave while we were there. We knew she had not yet fully achieved the emotional maturity to handle the idea that the watering of the ground above where her brother lay did not harm him in any way.

Shortly before we went there, I realized it was imperative that she begin to understand the concept of "no feeling." It seemed to me that the ultimate horror to a young child would be that her brother was lying in the ground with all that dirt and grass on top of him—not to mention water from a sprinkling system seeping down.

To explain "no feeling" I began a few days before her first

visit to discuss the difference between alive and dead. I asked her to take a strand of her hair and to yank it. She did and it hurt.

"That is because your hair is alive at the root," I told her. "Now, take that same strand of hair, hold it at the bottom with one hand and halfway up the strand with the other. Pull the part between as hard as you can and you will see it does not hurt. That is because your hair is dead and has 'no feeling' except at the root because that is alive."

She was able to grasp graphically what a million words could not have explained. We frequently reminded her of the "no feeling" idea and gradually she came to understand that to be dead meant not to feel hot or cold or pain or fear. It meant not to feel. Anything.

In the Jewish faith, following the funeral, we have a seven-day period of intensive mourning called shiva during which time prayers are offered and people are encouraged to visit and to bring food to the bereaved family. Our house was nearly always filled, and without question we found this most helpful and therapeutic.

We did not suffer the sudden silence and emptiness people frequently experience after the funeral. When we needed to talk about our son we had many sympathetic ears and they were necessary. The time immediately after the funeral was a period when we talked with people and ate with people. The major drawback to this outpouring was that we spent less time with our son than he needed and we did not discover this until sometime later.

It is most common for friends of a bereaved family to feel the family needs to be alone with its thoughts and hurt. While some privacy is essential, being alone with my thoughts after the funeral was the last thing in the world I needed. People were called for and people we got. There was conversation and even laughter. Yes, I took part in the laughter too because grief —profound and far-reaching as it is—is not total. It can only be sustained for so long in a given stretch of time.

Also, I did not feel the least discomfort in crying before a roomful of caring friends and family.

Contrast this sharing of sorrow with one couple whose son died of a kidney ailment. Though a good number of people turned out for the funeral, the couple, who were now childless, went home afterward to a bleak and empty house. The mother, dazed and bewildered, said she walked back and forth in the kitchen unable to quite figure out how to get a meal together. They sat there, the two of them, alone and grieving. Not because they were without friends—after all, many people came during visitation times at the funeral parlour—but because friends mistakenly thought the couple needed time. During bereavement—especially in the beginning—time is always there. What is needed is a break in time.

Offering consolation after the funeral is something that has bedevilled well-meaning friends and family throughout the ages.

What to say, how best to help.

Just be there. Not only at the beginning, but later. Grief is not automatically cut off after a "respectable" interval. It is a long-term anguish.

Many newly bereaved parents may disagree with a certain very strong reaction of mine but because I have found a number of others who shared my response, it seems worth mentioning.

People, out of the deepest compassion and kindness, felt that donations to the Heart Association would be a suitable memorial to my son. I am sure the feeling these people wished to express was one of "so that he did not die in vain." But in those early days filled with anguish and bitterness and despair at the irretrievable loss of our son, my concern for others who might be helped by such memorials was almost nil. Many bereaved parents faced with the same kind thoughts from others felt much the same way. However, since such donations are appreciated by some, when suggestions of memorial contributions are announced at a funeral or stated in an obituary notice, it is constructive to follow the family's wishes.

Grieving is a time of selfness. There is little that is altruistic about it. I have felt ashamed of my reaction to the kind and good intentions of countless donors. I thought myself lacking in gratitude when I should have felt thankful. Many parents have assured me they felt the same way.

It was only later that I appreciated these memorials.

Instead, my only feeling when opening the daily mail and its outpouring of donation cards was to think, "So what? Robby is dead. I do not really care how much research is done now. It is too late. It just doesn't matter any more."

It took much time for me to review those donations and accept them for what they were: kind and considerate tributes from people who only wanted to do something to help.

For those of you who felt resentment and are ashamed of it, take comfort in knowing you are not some ungrateful creature unworthy of being treated kindly. You are not alone. You are human and others have experienced what you felt.

Of course, many bereaved parents look upon such tributes without frustration. They feel less bitterness. Less hurt. Less anger. They think not of where the money is going but rather of the kindness shown by caring people. Certainly their example is the more wholesome.

Now, some years later, with my life back in focus, it pleases me to know that somewhere there may be a parent who will not have to endure what I went through because people gave generously when Robby died.

Those first days immediately following the death of a child are most unsettling because of the strange mixture of anguish and numbness most bereaved parents experience. But life does go on and the taking of certain steps cannot be avoided indefinitely.

While there are many parents who took great pride in the beauty of the funeral service in which their child was buried—they appreciated the pomp and ceremony and dignity—some parents feel none of the ceremonials helped. Perhaps a word, phrase, or parable penetrated their grief, but mostly it is viewed as a hurdle—something to be gotten through.

The important thing to remember is, the funeral is done and over and behind you, so do not compound the problems of rebuilding your life by feeling regrets over things you wish had been done differently.

*When your parent dies you have lost
your past. When your child dies you
have lost your future.*

—DR. ELLIOT LUBY

BEREAVEMENT AND GRIEVING

To bury a child is to see a part of yourself, your eye colour, your dimple, your sense of humour, being placed in the ground. It is life's harshest empathetic experience and must therefore be the hardest one with which to deal. In reality, when children die, not only are we mourning *them*, we are also mourning that bit of our own immortality that they carried.

A poem written by Herbert Parker most graphically explains the enormity of the bereaved parent's "loss of future":

> *His little arms crept 'round my neck
> And then I heard him say
> Four simple words I shan't forget—
> Four words that made me pray. . . .
> They turned a mirror on my soul,*

23

On secrets no one knew.
They startled me, I hear them yet;
He said, "I'll be like you."

Although studies of the grieving process are by no means complete, psychiatrists in general agree there are certain normal reactions.

The first sensation a parent has at the news that his child is dead is one of numbness, a sense of not actually being the bereaved party. I recall feeling, that terrible time in Alabama, that none of this was real. It was not actually happening and certainly not to me. It is almost the sensation of having an injection of novocaine in your gums. You can hear the dentist drilling and yet you feel nothing. It is as if the dental procedure was happening to someone else.

I will never forget the name of the doctor who told us our son was dead—or his face. Also indelible is the look on the face of the young nurse who stood by us when we were told. Wherever we glanced we saw only pitying faces and some faces that turned away.

The numbness stayed with me for days and would come in waves just as my weeping and sorrow would come in waves. For that, a grieving parent can be thankful. If we had to face the enormity of our loss for every waking minute, I am certain it would completely envelop us and consume us and prevent us from ever again becoming whole.

During the week after Robby's death, I recall a strange—for me—feeling of acquiescence. If someone told me to sit, I sat. If I was told to eat, I ate. A normally strong-minded person, my behaviour then was certainly atypical. I appreciated, in fact, being told what to do. I was too numb to wish to think for myself. Conversely, I was afraid the numbness would leave—and make way for grieving.

Having suffered for many years from sleeplessness, I found

my problem was compounded after Robby died. In my normal pattern, nothing is more pleasurable than reading a good murder mystery at bedtime. After the funeral, however, I stopped reading them. There was that frozen fear that I would read about death—the last subject which I wanted to think about. Instead, I would lie awake. Finally I began using sleeping pills, which helped considerably because my physical exhaustion undermined much of my coping ability. The only problem with sleeping pills was the determined effort it took to break myself of the habit.

Worst of all, far worse than lying awake all night, were the mornings. There seemed to be daily a brief period shortly after I opened my eyes when I completely forgot Robby was dead. Then, like a tidal wave, remembrance would come and engulf me and make me feel as if I were drowning. I had to fight my way out of bed every day—and I mean every day. This went on for several months and was probably my toughest battle. Nothing in life can be more emotionally draining than struggling to leave one's bed. If it takes all that much to get up, what energy is left for the rest of the day?

Another reaction, and one I remember most clearly, was my inability to concentrate on anything for any length of time. Things I had always taken for granted as my normal healthy "escapes" were suddenly taken from me. No longer could I become absorbed in a book, although I had been a voracious reader from early childhood. Television seemed more insipid than ever. Good movies were few and far between. Conversations with friends could hold my attention for only a short while.

During that time, I suppose my primary feeling was one of detachment. Nothing that was alive and part of this world was real. The only reality I knew was, Robby was dead. That was truth. Everything else was false.

Gradually, though, the detachment left. In its place came

pain. Deep, slashing, gouging pain that knifed through me with only brief periods of respite. Strangely, with this pain, I believe, came the beginning of healing. It was during this time that I stopped being buffeted by the suggestions of others and decided to go back to thinking for myself. It seemed what numbness could not do, pain could. It brought me physically back to this world—the world of the living. I stopped thinking that only death was real. I began to recognize that I was alive, and that was very real.

Although getting up in the morning still presented a giant problem, once I got out of bed the pain I felt acted like a glass of cold water dashed on a fainting person. It woke me up and I realized I would have to face the day, deal with my other two children, my son Dale, twelve, and my daughter Stacie, four, and cope with life.

This attempting to cope with life meant different things to me than to my husband. Nowhere in all the annals of sex discrimination is there a more glaring injustice than that thrust upon a bereaved father.

My husband was a victim.

Here was a man, a father, who watched his child being buried and according to convention was asked by society to "keep a stiff upper lip." Demands upon him began from the time the doctor in Alabama initially asked him to come into the conference room when our son died. The doctor, certainly with no idea other than to comfort in the worst possible situation, instinctively felt Robby's mother needed to be told more gently than Robby's father.

In the months to come, my husband discovered these demands upon him were universal—and very unfair. He went to the funeral parlour to make burial arrangements. He selected the clothes in which Robby would be buried. At no time was I asked to participate in any of the macabre arrangements the living must make for the dead. The atmosphere around us was one of comfort for me and "certain things must be faced" for my husband.

Along with all the affairs of dying he was also required after a while to earn a living. He is a salesman whose job requires continual self-motivation. It is impossible to tell just what the demands of society cost him in full, but one thing is certain. He paid dearly for maintaining a stiff upper lip.

As time went on, instead of coming out of his state of grieving, he sank deeper and deeper into sorrow.

"I feel as if I am walking across the Arctic snowcap," he would tell me. "I am very tired. I know if I lie down to rest I will fall asleep. I know if I fall asleep I will freeze to death. I just don't care. I can't fight my tiredness any more."

This is how the man felt inwardly as he faced the world "bravely" each day and shook hands with customers and made new contacts. He walked around wondering when it would be his turn to grieve.

Finally, he reached a point where we both knew he needed psychiatric help. He does not remember getting much help or guidance. But, and maybe this is what it was all about, he spent any number of sessions crying. Just crying.

Only after many such psychiatric meetings did he begin to feel he had left the snow-covered Arctic. To this day, though, he can still recall his emotions and, when he does, he shudders at the bleakness he had discovered within himself.

Not all people are fortunate enough to come out of this period intact. Stories abound in which a parent suddenly takes on a new behaviour in seeking thrills that would excite a teenager rather than an adult. Although I advocate happiness I do not advocate hedonism. As in other facets of living and dealing with problems, extreme reactions bring about their own sets of problems.

The man who became a stunt motorcyclist after his son died in an automobile mishap or the mother who left her husband and became an exotic dancer after their only child died left behind them hurt partners and families.

Other parents do not go seeking thrills. Instead, their reaction is the opposite. They become fearful and feel the need to wrap those they love even closer to them.

One suburban woman, although her child died from a physical ailment, suffered terribly whenever her surviving youngsters went off to play outside.

Another mother, whose son was a drowning victim, will not allow her children—or her husband—anywhere near a swimming pool or lake. "I just can't handle my fear. It's not worth their few hours of pleasure when I have to undergo such terror. They don't even argue with me about it. I guess they understand," the woman explained.

All too often, however, children faced with such restrictions do not understand. They strain to break free from bonds which they find unreasonably constricting.

One twelve-year-old girl confided she hates her mother from June to September because summer becomes a time of "you can't do this or that."

"I don't care if my brother died when his rowboat tipped. I have a right to swim and go to the beach. He's been dead two years and I'm left with no one to play with during vacation. She won't even let me go to camp!"

As in many other steps of the bereavement process, if it appears to be impossible to allow a normal life to go on around you and with you, perhaps professional guidance should be considered. Of course, what is normal varies, but some people deal with death in a manner that guarantees no one around them will ever be free of grieving.

One mother who lives in a small suburban bungalow has

turned her dead son's bedroom into a virtual shrine. More than a year has passed since he was killed in an automobile accident, yet his school books sit on his desk as if he will return anytime to continue his education. His bed remains unmade, just as he left it. A half-empty soda-pop bottle still sits on his dresser.

"His room will remain untouched as long as I live," his mother said. "I believe this way, my way, is right. This is how my child should be remembered."

The unfairness of this enshrinement concept is that the other children who are alive are made to feel they must tiptoe reverently about their home. When they complain about the atmosphere in which they live, they do so not from imagination but from the nearly palpable gloom that hangs over the very air in their home.

We all loved our dead children and carry a special place for them within us, but beyond a picture in a special place, a time of memorial, perhaps a special remembrance at birthday time or a visit to the cemetery, it is unfair to those alive and trying to cope to create a tomblike environment at home.

There are many bereaved parents who rightly or wrongly believe doctors did an inadequate job of caring for their children. In these parents hatred festers. They have often taken this most negative emotion and forced it upon surviving children.

One such case is the brother of a youngster who died of an obscure disease which doctors were unable to detect until it was too late to save the child. Not only are the parents embittered against a particular doctor, they have passed on their hatred of him to the surviving brother. Fifteen years after his ten-year-old brother died, he speaks venomously of this doctor.

Probably all too common among parents who develop reactions out of the normal range of grieving are those who begin to experience physical ailments either real or imagined. Sometimes the ailments take on the form of what caused the death of their child. Physicians and family should take a long hard look at such ailments and recommend counselling.

And, of course, some parents completely withdraw from society. Although each extreme bereaved response is tragic, it would seem this is the most hopeless because the parents have removed themselves from the prime source of easing their hurt —the company of their fellowman.

Many of the negative patterns, unfortunately, are set during the weakest time—the most vulnerable time—for these parents. They are set during the early stages of grieving.

Methods people use in coping—or trying to cope—with grief are as highly personalized as people themselves. Not every solution is right for every parent. Some things, however, can apply to most people.

The easiest, and in the early stages the most necessary, method is to roll with the punches. The parent who has suffered this tremendous shock should allow the waves of grief to submerge him or her, but he also should allow the tide of momentary forgetfulness to sway him gently for the few precious moments it is present.

One of the most essential ingredients for a father in coping with his grief is to forget all about that good old Anglo-Saxon ethic of stoicism and to cry. Let the tears come. Let them flow. They help wash away sorrow.

It is during this early period, even though the pain is great, that we must begin to take the first steps out of the cocoon of mourning and back into the land of the living.

Although in no way should your grief be buried, it is important to take some positive steps. Do it slowly, trying to be gentle with yourself.

For a mother, such a step could be something as simple as putting on lipstick or changing a hairstyle. One of my earliest affirmative steps in that grieving time was to decide one day, three months after Robby's death, to bake a cake for dessert instead of serving the usual store-bought pastry. It actually hurt while I baked that first time and I attempted nothing else for about a week. Then, one night, I set the table with a cloth instead of slapping down a few plates. I whipped potatoes instead of throwing frozen french fries into the oven. I prepared a roast instead of hot dogs. The real success of this second attempt was that the following night I was able to serve another decent meal.

Many men agree with taking this conscious first step. A teacher whose married son died, in Vietnam did it when he took his third-grade class on an unscheduled field trip. A fireman whose nine-year-old boy had died of pneumonia talked to some touring children at the firehouse instead of turning away from them. A businessman ate lunch at a restaurant with friends instead of brown-bagging it alone in his office.

Interestingly, these people all remember that first small step. Many faltered. Most came home and cried or brooded. Often, they did not attempt anything again for a short period of time. But the feeling that there was perhaps still something left to enjoy penetrated their grief.

It is important that no one neglect taking that first small step—and it should be a small one. That way, if you fall, it's just a tiny way down. It won't be terribly hard to climb back up again.

It's something you can do.

*Often the test of courage is not to die
but to live.*

—ALFIERI

BEREAVEMENT AND GUILT

Not too long ago, a young woman whom we will call Laura walked into a big city police station and told the desk sergeant she had killed her baby. He arrested the tall, thin, white-faced woman and she was eventually ordered to appear at a preliminary hearing on a charge of murder.

Laura, in her confession, explained to police she had smothered her infant daughter six years before and her crime had gone undetected. Now, she was ready to pay for what she had done.

The wheels of justice ran their normal course. She was held in jail where she sat uncomplaining until her court date. But once in court a strange thing happened. No one who knew Laura—and that included her former husband—believed a word of her confession.

As it happened, in my capacity as a reporter, I was assigned to cover the story and Laura's trial. After listening to the circumstances surrounding her child's death as outlined by the police, as well as speaking to her family, I became convinced Laura's child had not been the victim of foul play but rather had died of sudden infant death syndrome, commonly called cot death. This type of death annually kills about ten thousand American babies aged three weeks to five months. In most instances, the baby, seemingly healthy, is put to bed and discovered dead of no apparent cause some hours later. Doctors currently are working with the theory that death is caused by a noninfectious virus.

Laura was very fortunate that the court appointed a conscientious man to act as her attorney. Like myself, he began to question whether his client had indeed killed her baby. Querying doctors, he insisted on a complete psychiatric work-up for her.

Even now, several years after her trial, the attorney, who has specialized in criminal law for twenty-five years, remembers Laura very clearly, primarily because of her ambivalence.

"She was the most passive client I have ever defended," he said. "It was almost as if she was disinterested in the proceedings. She made absolutely no demands upon me. She never insisted on having her 'rights' protected as most clients do. She just sat there and everything was 'all right' as far as my handling the case was concerned."

At her trial, Laura stood thin and drawn, clad in blue jeans and a white blouse. Her face was pale and she had such a blank look in her eyes that it was almost painful to see. Her family was present and gave evidence as to how devoted a mother she was. Her former husband, from whom she had parted with some bitterness and who had subsequently remarried, testified that she was a good mother and in his opinion incapable of killing the daughter she adored.

Yet Laura told police she had picked up a pillow and smothered the child. The case against her was ultimately dismissed when the post mortem was admitted as evidence. It clearly indicated the child was not smothered.

Nearly as tragic as the misguided confession was Laura's reaction to the dismissal of charges against her. Although tears ran down her cheeks, her eyes still held their dead vacant look. Her lawyer believes it just wasn't enough for the courts to exonerate her. Laura would continue to feel responsible for her child's death until she could purge herself of her feelings of self-blame. He said that while researching for her defence he came across several similar examples of parents who were convinced they killed their babies but actually had not.

His view was substantiated in a study of the psychiatric toll of the sudden infant death syndrome, in which some letters from deeply anguished parents were included. In one letter, a mother told everyone she had smothered the child, despite a coroner's report to the contrary.

Psychiatrists say this is a fantasy that cannot be resolved until the person is willing to explore why he feels the death was his fault.

Since in crib death there is no visible cause, almost always there is a police inquiry. Regardless of how the questions are asked, whether gently by an understanding officer or perhaps more brutally, the result of the police contact is an intensification of the parents' feeling of guilt.

In general, according to the infant death study, psychiatric personnel have found an autopsy can be concrete assistance to parents trying to cope with the death of their seemingly healthy infant. An autopsy report can ease anxieties about whether or not they were careless. It can ease fears about whether the baby choked due to their lack of proper attention. Parents sometimes even fear the baby cried itself to death, and express guilt because they failed to look in on the child. None of these fears is usually grounded in fact, but that does not make it less real or less painful to parents unable to shake their guilt feelings.

An unfortunate aspect of crib death is the fear parents experience if they have another baby. One mother said she watched her second child like a hawk until the child was two years old—well beyond the cot-death danger period, as she certainly knew. She simply could not relax until the baby safely passed what she considered a hazardous period. She says she slept only fitfully if at all during the night, was irritable and exhausted around her husband and is just now becoming convinced her baby will live.

One explanation for the unfounded self-blame by crib-death parents is what can be best described as a broad cultural guilt. We have been taught from infancy that parents love children. Nowhere in the idealized version children are given of parenting are they told mothers and fathers can love their offspring and still at times feel anger and resentment toward them.

Yet, in nearly all families these emotions are felt.

The founder of a centre for the study of death and dying points out there is some anger in all loving relationships. Perhaps with a baby anger is a result of having one's freedom curtailed or being awakened out of a sound sleep to feed the infant. This certainly is not an unusual emotion. But should the child die, this resentment, which was certainly not unfounded and was well within the bounds of a normal parent-child relationship, turns to self-blame.

From there, a parent will sometimes become convinced the child died because the parent felt such negative things as resentment and annoyance.

"After all," such a parent might think, "It was wrong of me to feel anger or annoyance even though the baby would wake me just as I had finally fallen asleep. I guess I didn't love my baby enough, or the 'right' way."

Psychiatrists claim such tortuous thinking is not at all uncommon in a bereaved parent.

Guilt as defined by Webster is the act or state of having done a wrong or committed an offense. Since all people sin, err, think bad thoughts, lie occasionally, or commit other assorted misdeeds large and small, there are times all of us can feel guilty. But when a child dies, unless we allow room for logic, such misdeeds can serve as a starting point upon which to blame oneself for the death.

One man, who went through his own personal hell after his son died, felt his experience in the area of guilt was so important to share that he volunteered his story with the understanding that his privacy would be respected.

"You know, it probably starts with the Ten Commandments," he told me. "Where it says 'Thou shalt not commit adultery.' I guess that's a basic tenet of every faith and it is taught to you as a kid. You are not supposed to break the commandments. When you get married you swear to forsake all others too. But my wife and I just couldn't make it as well as I thought we would and I began playing around. Then our son developed cancer. I watched his agony and couldn't handle it. Aside from seeing someone I loved in pain, I began to believe my son—my only boy—was suffering because I had sinned. God was punishing me. When my boy died, I just could not be comforted. Or, rather, I would not let myself be comforted because I felt responsible for what happened. My smoking went up to three packs a day and I couldn't tell my wife why I became even more distant than before. I finally reached the point where I felt I was cracking up and I went to a psychiatrist. It took three years of twice-weekly sessions for me to understand I wasn't responsible for my boy's death. I can live with it now and I understand he didn't die because of me. But sometimes when I am very blue or tired the thought creeps back into my mind. When it does I pull myself up short and go back to thinking logically. One thing, though, my wife and I are close again and I have stopped cheating."

One woman in a small town bore an illegitimate child some thirty years ago and, instead of giving it up for adoption, as was commonly done then, she kept the girl and reared her in the face of society's criticism. Well, the mother eventually married, as did the daughter. But the daughter died soon afterward following gall-bladder surgery. It has been two years and the mother still regards her daughter's death as a punishment for her "sin." Wiped out completely from her mind are the years of love and caring she gave the child. All she can think now is that her daughter died because the mother had engaged in premarital sex.

These parents are victims of an idea implanted in most of us from early childhood. That idea is magical thinking. As children we are taught to pray or wish for things very hard and as a reward if we are very good our prayers or wishes will be granted. If we behave properly Santa Claus far away at the North Pole will know about it and reward us. The tooth fairy will place money under our pillows. After all, couldn't Cinderella's fairy godmother really be ours and grant wishes? Pray to God and if you are very good He will answer your prayers.

Spending a lifetime with this idea, we are grounded in the notion that our wishes and our deeds have some bearing on major events. While this can be true in most human endeavours, it is rarely the case in matters of life and death.

We may wish for a new car or home and take the steps necessary to acquire them. We may wish for a summer vacation, a winter ski trip. We may wish for happiness or love. In many instances we have it within our power to take the necessary steps whether they be at work or in our social lives to bring about the things for which we hope.

But generally in life-and-death matters we are stymied. Here in this most crucial of all things we find ourselves powerless to achieve what we want. My prayers were not answered. Neither were those of countless other parents who have buried their children. I was lucky because I did not view this as a judgment upon me.

There are any number of tragic cases, however, where bereaved parents feel just that. They are convinced their own sins set the stage for their child's death. Promiscuity, adultery, underhanded financial dealings, a lack of belief in God—in short, any breaking of the Ten Commandments with which most of us are imbued can set up obsessions that can lead to disaster if a child dies.

Often, too, an expert claims, parents pass a self-imposed judgment that is not a function of the situation.

One such example concerns the father who had quarrelled with his son over a dirty garage and an unmade bed and the boy's failure to do his schoolwork. In general, a most unsatisfactory morning passed between the two. Three hours later, the boy was dead, the passenger in a car hit by an oncoming truck at a busy intersection.

The father for several years was unable to come to terms with his own lack of culpability in his son's death. After all, he had felt both anger and resentment toward his son. And parents, he reasoned, are not supposed to feel that way. Therefore the boy died because of the father's hostility. It was all the father's fault.

Again, magical thinking.

Some parents carry a load of guilt that is fostered by the role of "protector" placed upon them by society and their "failure" to fill that role.

One such case is that of a young boy who drowned while his parents were painting a summer cottage. They had left him in charge of a baby sitter, a usually competent young woman, who turned away from her charge for a few minutes to chase the family dog that had gotten loose. While she was gone, the boy went into water over his head and she found him floating, dead.

The parents have since sold their cottage—a source of pleasure for them and all four of their surviving children—and seem unable to stop blaming themselves.

Unless there are extenuating and deep-seated guilt feelings, it is easier to cope with a child's death from a physical ailment than from an accident.

One psychiatrist maintains parents are often able to regard heart disease, leukaemia, or bone cancer, for example, as foreign invaders over which they had no control. They frequently can more readily accept the fact that they were not to blame for the death than can the parents of a child who died accidentally. An accidental death, he believes, often leads parents to question whether they should have given Jimmy the car that night, allowed him to take the boat out, or not allowed him to ride his bicycle in the street. With a death such as cancer, parents feel they are victims too because they have endured the pain of watching the child suffer.

In other words, when a child dies by accident, parents are likely to feel guilty because of their poor decision-making. But we more readily recognize our lack of control over disease.

If my own experience is an example, the psychiatrist is quite correct. While I have experienced grief and powerlessness and made mistakes in dealing with my *surviving* children, I seem to feel no recognizable guilt with regard to my son's death. This may be the case in part because of the careful handling we received from our paediatrician.

He always believed in honesty when it came to dealing with parents of very ill children. He explained in the early stages of our ten-year fight for our son that real medical practice is not what we see on television. There, doctors keep secrets from parents. He warned us early that the chances of Robby's survival were not great. Perhaps fortunately in the long run for me, I took his warning seriously and believed this terrible thing —that our son could die—was possible.

The doctor and I made a pact whereby he promised to tell me when to worry if I would promise to try not to worry when he felt it was unnecessary. Although at times it was very painful, after a while I came to believe in his honesty, and when he told me I did not have to be afraid during a certain stage in a given illness, I came to accept his word and it held good right to the end. Therefore, while doing everything medically and physically possible for him, I was fractionally able to prepare myself mentally for Robby's death. I remember consciously thinking I must do certain things—including punishing him for misbehaving in order to give him as normal a childhood as possible—to avoid regrets if he should die.

Another expert in dealing with sick children was our son's cardiologist. He frequently stressed giving as much normalcy— and its accompanying by-product of security—as was possible.

I credit in large measure my lack of feeling unjustified guilt to having followed their advice. I take comfort in knowing my son had as normal a childhood as his poor health and its frequent incursions upon his life would allow.

Perhaps no parent can match the pain of guilt with the feelings of those whose child has committed suicide.

Where did I fail? How did I fail? Could I have prevented this? What kind of person can I be if my own child would do this to get away from me? I didn't pay enough attention. I paid too much attention.

All these guilt-ridden thoughts run through the minds of parents when a child commits suicide.

Rarely, without therapy, does a parent think: Where did *he* (the child) fail? How did *she* fail? Could *he* have prevented this? What kind of person could *she* have been, and so on.

Dr. Bruce Danto, psychiatrist and head of Detroit's Suicide Prevention Center, says that, along with the feelings of guilt, there is an unconscious resentment toward having been electively and publicly abandoned by a son or daughter who, in the minds of the parents, catastrophically showed that their love was not enough.

In his work with parents who must learn to deal with a child's voluntary death, Dr. Danto claims group interaction between people who have undergone similar experiences is most beneficial. Also, he maintains, people should work at overcoming the socially unacceptable idea of speaking ill of the dead.

"In effect, someone who kills himself has copped out," he says.

Danto claims siblings suffer more when a brother or sister has committed suicide than from any other death because they too feel guilt and personal failure.

"Kids are the most lied-to group of people next to the Internal Revenue Service," he says. "Rather than grieving and working out the problems as a family, they are generally shunted away and almost never told the truth."

He says it is not inappropriate to be angry with the dead, especially when trying to understand suicide at the same time you try to explain it to your surviving children.

Although he cautions you must always know your child before offering any explanation, he says there is nothing wrong with telling the straight truth. He suggests that adding some of your own speculations as to why the child opted for this calamitous way out may be of benefit. That speculation should not take on a tone of blame upon survivors, of course. "He was a loner. She was unhappy. It was beyond our power to make him happy no matter how hard we tried. She did a rotten thing."

Dr. Danto insists there is nothing wrong with feeling anger when someone has taken such an "unfair" way out.

The theory here is to nip in the bud as many guilt feelings as possible and to remove areas of personal fault-finding. The main thing in dealing with the surviving family members of a suicide is to keep an open exchange. Don't suppress the expression of legitimate negative feelings about your child if he committed suicide.

One couple whose son shot himself has worked through many problems. What has not been handled is the feeling that had he been disciplined more firmly as a child, he might not have gone to drugs and ultimately to his death. But it is important for every parent to remember that if we were intended to function with perfect hindsight our eyeballs would be at the backs of our heads. When a child is dead, it is imperative to remember just where our eyeballs are located. Hindsight does no good for the dead child. Things can no longer be undone. Therefore it is nothing more than an exercise in futility.

Reviewing mistakes is of less than no value when reliving the time spent with your now dead child, unless you can use some new-found knowledge in rearing other children. A caution here which cannot be overlooked: Beware of the backlash your grief may unleash. If you were too strict with the dead child do not suddenly become so liberal that all rules are suspended. The same is true in reverse.

People logically should not blame themselves for things they did not know they were mishandling. But when a child dies of suicide or by the use of drugs, it is almost impossible not to think about what could have been done differently.

It is almost inevitable for mothers and fathers to experience a sense of having failed in such cases. Whether the child took to drugs because of peer pressure or to escape reality—or even because he or she was convinced of the immortality of one's youth—parents almost always think: What could we have done differently? It is essential for parents faced with this tragedy to disabuse themselves of this idea, this sense of having failed. Not everything is within our control. Often things are beyond our handling, our coping, our correcting. Try to understand and accept the concept that perfect parenting is a role beyond realistic human capability.

It may help to remember: "I did the best I was able to do in the job of rearing my child. I had no training and by trial and error I did the best I could." Remember, too, a person's "best" may vary from day to day depending on life's other pressures and involvements.

When trying to overcome unjustified guilt, just as in many areas of bereavement, a compassionate third ear can lend enormous support. Not all of us have had the benefit of guiding doctors, nor can we always seek psychiatric counselling, but nearly everybody has a friend or relative or neighbour to speak with. Find a person—and do not constantly alternate the person—whose judgment you trust. You will probably discover that the feedback you get will enable you to see more clearly that your child did not die because you sinned, were neglectful, or were a bad parent. You may even discover, if you really choose to delve, why you feel guilty for an event, so tragic, that you did not bring about.

*But tell not Misery's son that life is
fair.*

—H. K. WHITE

BEREAVEMENT AND POWERLESSNESS

There is an old Syrian legend that tells of a beautiful youth, the son of the sultan, who dashed into his father's place in Damascus crying that he had to leave immediately for Baghdad.

When the sultan asked the lad why he was in such haste the boy replied, "I just saw Death standing in the palace garden, and when he saw me, he stretched out his arms as if to threaten me. I must lose no time in escaping him."

Agreeing, the sultan gave the boy his swiftest horse. When he left, the ruler angrily stalked into his garden and demanded to know of Death how he dared to intimidate the son of the sultan.

Death listened, astonished, and answered, "I assure you I did not threaten your son. I only threw up my arms in surprise at seeing him here because I have a rendezvous with him tonight in Baghdad."

The sultan, the most powerful man in his country, knew then what bereaved parents have since learned. There are certain things we are powerless to change.

Because the death of a child, and its accompanying feeling of powerlessness, go against the most basic of parental instincts—that of protecting our offspring—the burden this emotion places upon us is doubly great. Faced with such a catastrophic finality, we bereaved parents all too often believe we should have been able to avert the tragedy.

When the feeling of powerlessness sets in, we find ourselves in the sorry situation of having to deal not only with our bereavement but also with our inability to have prevented it.

We, who have not been spared much that is difficult, must also deal with this double emotion. Powerlessness is one of the true quagmires of grief that we will encounter and one of the most painful stages in coming to terms with grief. We can measure the importance of coping with powerlessness by the sheer weight of its difficulty.

Some psychiatrists claim bereaved parents approach powerlessness the same way they individually deal with any thwarting situation. Anger, rage, a sense of frustration, fear, weeping, hysteria. Powerlessness encompasses them all. They maintain also, because of the stress placed upon mothering and fathering by our society, that grieving over a child magnifies this sense of impotence more than any other death.

Even in the case of powerlessness, the roles men and women are expected to play have a part in how grief is handled. In many instances, the feeling of a lack of power to alter circumstances is a greater problem to a father than to a mother.

One upper-middle-income family nursed their daughter for nearly two years before she succumbed to cancer at the age of twelve. Despite nearly unlimited funds spent to save her, and the most tender and loving care, she died.

The parents have taken a concrete step toward coping with their grief—they are members of an organization of bereaved parents—but they have not yet come to terms with powerlessness. The man spends seven days a week at his office; his wife claims any number of physical ailments, which her doctors say are manifestations of her grief.

"It has been three years since our daughter died and I don't think I will ever accept it. I feel I should have been able to save her," said the father.

Many sociologists would agree that a man who has successfully worked and seen his efforts bear fruit financially is more accustomed to bending events to meet his wishes. That he was unable to control happenings surrounding the most important thing in his life—saving his daughter—might be quite difficult to accept for such a father. Indeed, such a dreadful occurrence would be difficult for any man because a father is a father regardless of his social and economic level.

While not usually possessed of business triumphs, a mother, too, still feels she should have been able to control her child's health.

From the time Robby was born weighing less than three pounds, doctors, although kind, never spared us the knowledge that we had a very sick child.

In the nearly ten years he lived, we fought fiercely to keep him free of infection, which was very wearing to his heart, and since I was the parent home with him, much of the war was waged by me. Toward the end, his life seemed to be an almost never-ending infection. He would go to school. Get sick. Stay home three or four days. Get well. Go to school and get sick again. For a decade trying to save our son became a prime reason for being.

And then, after nearly ten years, he died. Suddenly I had to face the fact that his death—the death of this child whom I loved so dearly—was beyond my control. I was bereft not only of Robby but of a way of life.

Oddly, and probably symbolically, I still recall most vividly his no-longer-needed bottle of digitoxin pills lying in the Alabama hotel room wastebasket. They were thrown there by a friend who was helping us pack our belongings so we could return to our home in Michigan. We had travelled hundreds of miles to give our son every chance for life because the leading surgeon for Robby's type of heart ailment was in Alabama.

We knew then even the best surgeon was just not enough.

I remember looking at that bottle and thinking that never again would I have to fight for him.

Like the pills never again to be taken, I felt from then on I too would be unused.

Psychiatrists maintain this feeling of powerlessness is present in all bereaved parents, but to varying degrees.

Perhaps the most powerless-feeling group of parents are those whose children's deaths resulted from accidents. Aside from the fact that any child's death leaves one with the feeling of utter pointlessness, an accidental death seems to bring about an intensified sense of futility.

Here we have a healthy and hopefully happy child who goes for a drive, swim, or bicycle ride and dies.

This is a youngster who left his home, probably yelled, "Bye, Mom. See you later," and simply never came home again.

Also, in contrast to our experience with a sick child, another group of parents who know powerlessness particularly well are those whose sons died because they were quite healthy—healthy enough to be drafted into the armed forces.

Imagine the feelings of a father or mother whose son died in Vietnam. Not only did they have to contend with grief, they also had to bear the anger over the war that was felt by many

Americans. These parents had a dead son while people insisted he had died in a useless, pointless, and immoral conflict. Waste? Futility? Lack of power to control events?

There are some parents, though, in this same situation, who are blessed with a strong sense of patriotism. Often it is strong enough to help tide them through the feeling of powerlessness.

"I loved my boy," said one father. "But I was proud when he came home in his army uniform. I knew there was a danger he could be killed. After all, people get killed in cars too. At least he did something with his life. He died for his country."

Another mother strongly disagrees with taking any comfort in that concept. A medical receptionist whose only son was killed in Vietnam, she has grown bitter. From a laughing friendly woman, friends say she has turned into a hostile person.

"Nothing is worth dying for when you leave people behind in such pain," she tells friends. "Nothing."

The woman spends much time and energy bemoaning the fact that she did not push her son to remain in college, thus deferring him from the draft. "We would still have him had I argued hard enough," she cries.

Still another set of parents who know the depths are those whose children die as a result of violence—an ever-increasing phenomenon in our society.

Imagine the shock felt by one elderly couple when they came face to face with the man found guilty of murdering their cabdriver son. The pair were Christmas shopping in a department store and happened to stand directly behind the man at a check-out counter. The husband who ran to the phone and called the prosecutor's office was told the killer was not an escaped felon. Instead, he had been declared sane by psychiatrists after a year in a state mental institution.

Another couple from an entirely different economic and social background feels just as intensely the sensation of powerlessness.

Their daughter's fellow high-school students had voted her the girl most likely to succeed. She had charm, intellect, and money. She was stabbed to death. The couple are certain their son-in-law did the killing, despite intensive investigation by police refuting this belief. They have hired private investigators to help prove their contention, but the investigators have turned up nothing to change the police view of the case.

The son-in-law abandoned his child, an eight-year-old girl, who was adopted by the grandparents.

"The thing we try hardest not to do, is fill her with hate," said the child's grandfather. "But we loved our daughter. We are certain he killed her and sometimes the hate seeps out. Try as we might not to let it show, I know that sometimes it does."

Most parents in this situation spend unlimited hours and days and years seeking an answer to why their child died. Some people, after exploring, find a religious significance to the death and are comforted. Others, if they really wish to survive, find ultimately they must stop asking why their child was a victim of brutality.

Perhaps the most frustrated father and the one whose experience has to rank as the epitome of powerlessness is the man who made national news in America when he protested the awarding, to his daughter's murderer, of a "Man of the Year" citation.

The recipient, who is in prison, had savaged, raped, and killed the father's married daughter nine years earlier. The community service organization was either ignorant of why their candidate was imprisoned or was convinced he had been rehabilitated, and honoured the convict for his work in translating forty-five thousand pages of book material into braille.

I remember what my own reaction—that of insensate anger —was upon reading the story, for my thoughts immediately flew to the dead girl's family.

The father of the dead girl, a widower, was given this mind-boggling news when his teen-aged son read it in a newspaper.

"Although it happened nine years ago, my boy has not gotten over the tragedy—he saw her body. Then, when he picked up the newspaper one morning and read that this creature was going to be the Jaycee man of the year," said the father, "he was beside himself. I called the newspaper and told the reporter who wrote the original story how angry and hurt I was that this could have happened. The outcome was, I appeared on three radio shows and answered many questions about how I felt. Nobody disagreed with me except the state organization. Our local chapter refused to go along with the award once they knew the facts.

"In spite of everything and my telling the media on radio and television and in the newspaper what kind of person was getting the award, they went ahead anyway."

"I didn't know how I would be able to stand this, but I believe in God and prayer. My only hope now is that God will punish him. Just being in jail is not enough. I am afraid this murderer will use the award to help get a parole, and that would be horrible."

The father gave me one additional bit of insight. As he waged his unsuccessful battle, he was bolstered with letters and phone calls from across the country from parents of children dead of varying causes, including disease, all speaking of the outrage they felt.

"One man who lives out-of-state called me four times and told me his son was murdered and I should fight this thing. The man really only wanted someone to listen to him cry. After his last phone call, I told him he would have to stop because I did not have the strength to listen to him and still fight my battle. I am nearly seventy years old. I felt bad but I had no choice."

Aside from the award ruckus, the father, who is now retired, said it was very difficult for him to come to terms with his daughter's brutal death, but his job helped him greatly.

"I worked and worked to help myself fight this thing," he said. "When I got home I did things around the house until I was so exhausted I would be asleep before I hit the bed. I had to be occupied all the time.

"I cried, too. Whenever people at work would come up to me and offer condolences I would start to cry. But it was something I had to get out of my system. Now to have this whole thing opened again and some sort of hero made of my girl's killer [who, according to the father, confessed in a letter he wrote him] is almost more than I can take."

As bereaved parents, regardless of the cause of our child's death, it is impossible not to empathize with what this man felt, the all encompassing powerlessness with its components of rage and frustration. Indeed, I recall my own anger when reading this "Man of the Year" episode.

When a child dies, the need in some of us to make some sort of statement, some refutation of our powerlessness, can be overwhelming.

One couple, although divorced, are taking legal action to avenge their son's death. If they are successful it could help alleviate their rage. According to the law suit, their teen-aged son developed influenza and was delirious. The mother claimed she contacted her family doctor who ordered the boy to go to a hospital where he would meet the boy.

The mother, according to a newspaper account, says the boy was in a semicomatose state and she was unable to dress him by herself and get him into her car. She called the police de-

partment of the suburban city in which she lived. A pair of pa-
trolmen arrived and decided the boy was not ill but suffering
from a drug overdose. They then strapped him to a stretcher
and instead of taking him to the hospital where his physician
was waiting, they took him to a drug facility, where he died.

Although no amount of money can bring back their dead
son, the parents are suing the police and the drug centre.

Whether or not they win the suit, it is only to be hoped they
will be able to work through some of their anguish. No matter
what the settlement—if there is one—the sad basic premise
will remain unchanged. Whether a court rules in their favour
or not, their son will be dead. A cash settlement or an apology
will be only a hollow victory when measured against the enormity of that truth.

Perhaps one of the most publicized examples of powerlessness was the death of the son of the late multimillionaire
Aristotle Onassis. The young man crashed and died in an airplane accident. Onassis's emotions could not have been much
different from those of some of the people I have described
when he offered a huge reward to anyone who could prove the
death was premeditated rather than an accident. Newspaper
accounts have speculated he never came to terms with his son's
death. There has even been discussion that his grief hastened
his death from myasthenia gravis, a disease that affects the
nervous system.

Conversely, as terrible as it is to understand you may have
no control over whether your child lives or dies, it is equally appalling to be given that choice.

According to an account in the Detroit *News*, one family did
not learn of their son's hydrocephalic condition until he was
two months old, when his head began to swell. The child had
been operated upon shortly after he was born to drain fluid
from the brain area. The parents were told at the time of the

recurrence their baby would never be more than an infant, never be able to comprehend anything.

The parents say they are bitter, and had they been told the truth at the child's birth they would never have consented to the original surgery. When he was two months old they decided not to allow doctors to reoperate. The child lived seven months, and his parents needed urgent psychiatric treatment to help cope with their trauma.

"It was the worst hell anyone can go through," said the mother. "It's something you need to discuss with someone. But in our society you can't discuss it because you're damned if you make this decision."

The baby's father is angry at such organizations as The Right to Life groups and others who would prevent them from making what they felt was a necessary decision.

"These groups come along and say, 'You've got no right to do this.' They don't know what they are dealing with."

"You learn from this kind of thing, though," he said.

"I wouldn't say that," interjected his wife. "You survive it."

These people were in a unique situation where they did have the power to decide whether their child should live or die, but that is not generally the case.

Most of us are not in such positions. We are confronted with wars, illness, or accidents when we lose a child. Usually we are horrified because we have to bow to things beyond our control.

Yet, having the decision taken from us is infinitely more simple. At least my mind can never torture itself over the question of whether it was moral to let my child die.

Parents such as this young couple have my deepest sympathy. Their anguish must be boundless, their burden almost too great for anyone to carry.

It is awful for bereaved parents to realize that nothing they can do or say can change the finality of their child's death. It becomes urgent, therefore, for such a mother or father to find something she or he can do—and, hopefully, do effectively.

The opposite of powerlessness, of course, is power. One of the basic things taken away from a bereaved parent is the conviction of possessing the ability to control, to have some say, in this world.

Feeling that ability is gone, a parent must turn elsewhere to believe once again in himself and to redevelop a sense of self-esteem, a sense that he still is capable, and has the right to function and make decisions.

If there is even the slightest value in protest or litigation—avenues to which some bereaved parents turn—it probably lies within a parent's once again believing he has some power. But parents taking this method of reestablishing themselves are in the minority.

Most of us try other ways of regaining our sense of self. We try to fight back by rebuilding our lives.

Sometimes we find a more creative approach to our jobs or our homemaking. Sometimes we throw ourselves into a new and challenging hobby. The proof of our own worth is very important after such a loss.

Some people experience an even greater exhilaration in achieving than that felt by those who have never lost a child. After such a soul-shattering nightmare, it is heady to create something, to bring something to life, to learn something new, to build something. It is probably all the more satisfying because it is such a long climb upward after fearing, when your child died, the highest you would ever reach again would be rock bottom!

Deceive not thyself by overexpecting
happiness in the married estate.

—THOMAS FULLER

BEREAVEMENT AND MARRIAGE

Perhaps one of the more difficult things to understand for someone who has not lost a child is the strange divisiveness that overtakes a marriage when the parents are bereaved.

"After all," an outsider would reason, "those two have been through the mill together. They have so much in common. They have shared all that sorrow. They probably never even argue after having undergone such a catastrophe."

That is how it looks on the surface but it just does not always work that way. Yes, they have shared tragedy, disaster, and grief, but these emotions do not necessarily create a tighter bond. Very often, instead of holding them together, the bond becomes so taut it snaps. In fact, some studies estimate that as high as 90 percent of all bereaved couples are in serious marital difficulty within months after the death of their child.

There are, of course, no universal answers as to why this

should be the case because every marriage is its own unique entity. But studies have shown there are threads of similarity in certain problems faced by parents of dead children.

And these studies have shown a common grief is not the best possible adhesive to cement a marriage.

Perhaps the basic reason for this lies in the fantasylike concept people have of marriage. Our culture has given us to understand that when a couple marry, two people are joined and become one. In many aspects this may well be true, but that ideal often shatters with the death of a child.

Suddenly, and frighteningly, this couple, this two wedded into one, has a basic truth thrust upon it. Once again they are two. Each must bear his or her own pain and a mate cannot bear it for you. Nor can a mate shield you from it. The couple, unlike when they laughed together, vacationed together, shared downfalls together, suddenly finds at the time of the greatest tragedy in their lives—and at the time of their greatest need—that each is an individual. They must mourn as individuals. Separately.

Anne Morrow Lindbergh, in her book *Dearly Beloved*, said, "Grief can't be shared. Everyone carries it alone, his own burden, his own way."

She was correct. But for a couple to discover this after burying their child can be shattering. After all, in the back of each of their minds, they believed they could lean on each other as they mourned. But you cannot lean on something bent double from its own burden.

What happens then is each parent finds himself on his own —and at what a time! Just when our expectations assured us we would have all sorts of support from a mate, we discover he is just about the last person who can really help. Society has conditioned us to believe we now would be one grieving pair. Instead we have become two bereaved people.

The magnitude of having this rug of expectation yanked out from under nearly destroyed my marriage.

During Robby's lifetime, we had done well in trying to comfort and cushion and support each other as we went from one crisis to another. I am convinced there is no one else with whom I could have withstood the innumerable alarms and dire death predictions. My husband says the same thing.

Yet, when Robby died, we suddenly found ourselves with a whole new set of circumstances. There was no longer any possibility of positive thinking. We could no longer tell each other that maybe all would be well.

Now we were left empty and without hope. Despite our two lovely children—and even they did not seem enough some of the time—the awful vacuum of death took us over.

Strange, in reflection, one of the ingredients that created a major problem was our mutual protectiveness. It did not take very long to understand, for either of us, that pouring our hearts out together was a destructive act of one to the other. We certainly did not wish to inflict further hurt. There would be times when I was having an "up" day and I would resent being pulled back into grieving. My husband felt the same way.

The strange combination of protectiveness and resentment created a chasm in our relationship that became one of the factors resulting in a brief separation and counselling. We both learned from the experience that we wished to stay married, but we would have to become more realistic in what we expected of each other. I could not expect him to be a tower of strength when his own grief was as great as mine. He could not expect me not to grieve in front of him even though it pulled him down.

We resolved it by setting aside a segment of time when we would bare our emotions. Also, our counsellor recommended I turn to some close women friends for comfort occasionally instead of my husband.

After all, the only thing anyone could offer was a sympathetic ear. There is nothing concrete anyone can do, anyone can say. That sympathetic ear need not necessarily be your mate's if he is resistant to your weeping. Your child is dead and no power can undo that. Whoever the listener is really makes no difference so long as there is sympathy.

Oddly, our problems never involved a difficulty common to many bereaved parents. Neither of us ever grew resentful when Robby's name was brought up. I have been assured our response was unusual.

In any number of families, according to psychologists, a highly divisive problem revolves around whether or not to discuss the dead child. They saw frequently—though by no means always—that it is the father more than the mother who tends to avoid these conversations. The reasons for this avoidance primarily by men are as complex as the whole spectrum of repression of grief that fathers often undergo. The stoicism, the insistence in our culture that men suffer in silence when faced with disaster, although slowly changing is still very much evident during bereavement.

Early in our grieving we made a pact that we would talk about Robby. He did exist. To avoid remembering him, to avoid discussing him, recalling his likes and dislikes, his character, his humour, seemed like letting him die twice. And this we simply would not do. We did not trammel each other's expectations when it came to listening about the living Robby. It was only the dead Robby that threw us for a loop.

There are couples, however, who are less fortunate. Usually, one mate will decide talking about the dead child is too painful to bear. Any attempt by a spouse to bring up the subject is met with anger, hostility, slammed doors. Anything to avoid the discussion.

Although moderation in this as in all things is desirable, it is necessary to talk about your child. You are in a state of mourning. If you were in the ocean you could not sidestep water. When you are grieving over the death of your offspring you cannot sidestep mentioning that child!

You should remember your child. You cannot bottle him or her away in a little corner of your mind never again to see the light of day. He was real. She existed. To close this memory off as if he or she never had been can be one of the most destructive things a parent can do. A mate can do.

The extreme, of course, can be equally destructive. There comes a time when it is also necessary to discipline your out-pourings of grief. To take hold of yourself. To stop crying incessantly. Not only can you cause unending pain to your spouse and surviving children, you will ultimately succeed in alienating everyone who makes up your life.

If you see you are at opposite extremes over this basic issue of your grieving with your mate, try to reach an agreement. Set up a time period daily, for example, when you both know it is time to talk about the child and when you will be listened to without encountering a hostile reception. It may even get him or her to talk after a while. And mourn. Remember, though, when that time period is over, force yourself with iron determination to step away from the topic. It can be done.

If you cannot reach a fair arrangement in this area, by all means seek outside help. You must learn to talk.

Learning to talk applies to many different phases of keeping your marriage intact although grieving.

If there were things at the funeral that you felt were wrong, even if done by your mate, do not harbour anger. Mention them.

But gently. Explain that you feel they were wrong *in your opinion.* Bring the issue out into the open and do not let it fester. As time goes on, the funeral diminishes in intensity and most often in importance if there is no lingering anger.

There are some areas of talking with each other—communicating—that are best left untouched, however, without the intervention of a third party.

I saw an example of how a situation fraught with the components of a complete marital breakdown was handled correctly in a group discussion conducted by bereaved parents.

An elderly couple whose married daughter had died asked for help in dealing with a son-in-law, recently remarried, who forbade them to see their grandchildren. Here were two people who verged on blaming each other for the difficulty with the man—and therefore the loss of their grandchildren—who were lucky enough to have a forum at which to present their problem. A serious one. After all, those youngsters were all they had left of their child.

They interrupted each other with asperity while describing the situation. It seemed he felt the woman had mistreated the new wife. The woman was convinced he had been nasty to the son-in-law.

Between them, their anger at being deprived of the grandchildren was almost tangible.

But, instead of brooding alone with these negative thoughts, they threw the subject open to a group of about thirty bereaved parents.

Questions were thrown at the pair.

"Did you get along with your son-in-law before?"

"Have you hinted at resentment of his new wife?"

"Have you made an extra effort to be nice to her?"

"Have you tried to instill in your grandchildren that their own mother was a better person, more attractive, kinder?"

The grandparents answered honestly and with not a trace of the vindictiveness they displayed to one another. Suggestions were made including one by a woman whose married son had died. She offered to call the son-in-law and help straighten out the problem by confronting the man and asking what was wrong.

Aside from this very concrete help, which was gratefully accepted, the meeting served another purpose. It became a defusing agent in an explosive situation.

The couple had been holding each other responsible for yet another loss besides that of their daughter. In their fear of losing, and desperate need to hang onto, what was left of her— their grandchildren—they were experiencing some rather dreadful feelings about each other.

"She doesn't act well to his new wife. She never makes an effort to call her. It's my wife's fault," the husband might have been thinking.

"He's just changed toward our son-in-law. He's almost rude. They used to build things together. Now, nothing. It's my husband's fault," might have flashed through the bereaved mother's mind.

But, in the group setting, questions were asked that were explicit about the relationship, yet kindly put by people with no stake other than to help two suffering human beings.

The discussion held before strangers who were nonaccusatory removed the tension that is frequently created when someone feels defensive. No one was pointing the finger of blame. Further, the group environment in this situation forced the two people to keep an open mind. It is rare that open animosity between husband and wife is expressed in these meetings. Instead, because there are others present, sympathetic others, parents tend to keep a rein on their angers and generally tend to absorb whatever help is offered.

While people certainly cry at these meetings they generally do not turn on one another and hurl hurtful comments at one another. Good manners usually prevent this from happening. And that is all to the good. If two people are not busy yelling, it is possible they will be able to hear something constructive.

Dr. Elliot Luby, chief of psychiatry at Lafayette Clinic in Detroit, has made a study of the behaviour and problems of bereaved couples. His research has enabled him to put forth a number of reasons for the foundering marriages in such families.

One basic problem, he said, is that parents, unable to understand how it could be that their child died, take to lashing out at their spouses. Indeed, each sometimes blames the other for the death.

"Why weren't you more careful?"

"Why did you let her take the car? Date that boy?"

"Why didn't you call the doctor?"

This blaming over the cause of death may appear ludicrous —the spouse is after all making what is tantamount to an accusation of the murder of their child to a vulnerable, susceptible mother or father. Just the mere hint of such a thing to grieving mates could be enough to make them believe they were indeed responsible for the death of their child. If in the back of the mind there is the least shred of doubt about personal judgment or responsibility, a question could be planted that would not be undone in a lifetime.

The reason, often, for this vindictive finger-pointing is the need to answer the basic question, why did their child die, and that question has never been answered since the beginning of time.

If you have the slightest inclination to blame your spouse, or if you personally feel responsible, seek immediate psychiatric help for yourself and your marriage. Because once that blame sets in, unless there is direct intervention, the marriage is nearly always beyond saving.

If a father is "convinced" his wife was responsible for the death of his beloved son, for example, the idea of maintaining a fulfilling and satisfying marriage is laughable.

If help is not sought and the problem not resolved, all hope of a meaningful life is nearly gone for both the blamed and the blamer.

One of the saddest couples I have seen were victims of this dreadful problem. Their young child died twenty years ago, when he ran in front of a car and was killed instantly. The husband, always an overprotective father, has never ceased blaming his wife for her "carelessness" while watching over their son. The wife was easily made to feel responsible for the death. Easily made to feel a murderer. Her defences were down anyhow because of the death of her child.

The wife, who had been rather a relaxed mother, left her child outside while she went to turn something off on the stove. She came back outside and her son was dead.

Before the tragedy, the couple had disagreed about how careful is too careful and how careful is not careful enough. Afterward, of course, it appeared the decision had been made. The child was dead. She had been wrong. She was responsible.

The two did not divorce. Instead, they live a nightmare. A hell. He, hating and physically ill. She, mentally ill. Oh, not bad enough to be hospitalized—she can still cook and clean—but bad enough to have retreated from society and her surviving children.

They are old now and never discuss their son or his death or anything else for that matter. All that is left is the residue of vindictiveness that hangs over their house like a layer of smoke.

Another destroyer in the marriage of bereaved parents appears to be the feeling that the union is star-crossed, doomed to endlessly face defeat and despair.

When that happens, bereaved parents sometimes find themselves in the position of the octogenarian couple who, after sixty years of marriage, sought a divorce.

"Why," asked the bemused judge, "would you even consider such a thing after all these years?"

The wife stood before the bench, leaning heavily on her cane, and replied, "Enough's enough!"

When two people feel things can only get worse, never better, what hope can there be for them as a unit? They are in effect living like the eighty-year-old couple. What such parents need is an infusion of logic by a third party, be it friend or professional. In such cases, unless there is intervention, these couples very often have convinced themselves, really convinced each other, that the only luck they can ever hope for is bad luck. All things bright and beautiful will be forever beyond them.

Someone trained or someone with a grain of sense and a better outlook can help such a couple overcome this attitude. Sometimes a fellow bereaved parent can fill this role.

When all is said and done, saving their marriage and making it whole again should be highly desirable to bereaved parents. After all, there is no one in all the world who can better understand the depths of the tragedy of their loss than the other person who experienced that loss. While this understanding is certainly not of itself enough to build a better marriage, it is something shared between them that needs no explaining.

My husband and I can hear a song, see a sight, meet a friend, and look at each other knowingly because somehow these things evoke a memory of Robby in both of us. It is a mutual experience and a wordless one. It is something special to have and something not to throw away until all avenues in trying to save the marriage have been explored.

Remember, a couple who can share a wordless experience, even a sad one, cannot really be called luckless, because they are not alone.

Although this communication is very special, not all couples can withstand the most unnatural pressures under which they find themselves. If they do divorce and, tragically, many bereaved couples do, they still may be able to offer reinforcement to each other. Sometimes the bitterness of the separation is insurmountable, and everything shared, including a common grief, is rent. Sometimes, however, the bitterness that caused the divorce dissolves once the marriage is over, and the two people, no longer bound by wedlock, are better able to help each other.

One former couple, each member now married a second time, is having great adjustment difficulties. She is a divorced bereaved mother who bears her new husband great ill will on occasion because "he just can't understand how I feel." Such couples must learn that in order to have a workable marriage they have to come to grips with this bereavement problem. I cannot strongly enough urge counselling in such situations. It is imperative that death not be pervasive enough to destroy a second union for such a bereaved mother.

There are couples who, alongside the terrible grief they suffer, also are confronted with vast medical bills from their child's terminal illness, which bills may never be paid in a lifetime. Bill collectors dun them. Frequently, they are in debt to friends and family. There is no money for clothing, barely enough for food, certainly precious little for "luxuries" like a movie to help relieve their grieving. In fact, the only prospects such people see are negative prospects.

One man, a factory worker who prided himself on never missing a day on the job, came to the end of what he could handle because of the money problems involved in his child's illness and the burial costs. He was so overwhelmed by the magnitude of never-ceasing hostile phone calls from people demanding money that he quit his job and left his family. They have not seen him in months. Meanwhile the phone calls go on. Only now, his wife bears the full brunt of them alone.

Money problems in our society are never nice. They are even worse when trying to fight your way up after burying a child. Solutions are often hard to come by.

When Robby was born two months prematurely, we had no hospitalization insurance. He was in intensive care for nearly three months and the cost for this specialized attention mounted astronomically daily. By the time he came home we owed medical bills totalling nearly ten thousand dollars! We were young, in our twenties, and saddled with debts that took years to repay because during Robby's life the bills kept increasing. There were points we were in so deep, surviving financially seemed impossible. This certainly did not help us cope with bereavement. Finally, we sought the services of a money-management counsellor who worked out a payment schedule with which we were able to live. He called our creditors, explained the problem, and established a plan that stopped the dunning calls.

There are other people, who, although wishing to be honourable about discharging their debts, find their only solution is filing bankruptcy or making reduced settlements with creditors.

When a couple find themselves in the financial muddle that only vast medical bills can bring, it is essential to seek some professional guidance. Unless someone who can take an overview of the entire money situation hauls you up short, you will find yourself merely putting your finger in a weakened dam.

You will pay whoever calls the most and yells the loudest without any reason or logic. Then you will find yourself getting angry letters and calls from someone who popped into the place of last month's most angry person.

It is not impossible to fulfill your financial obligations if you are working. It may take years, but with the aid of a marriage counsellor, money manager, lawyer, or financially sophisticated friend, it can be done. If you are in such difficulty, find help.

Another source of severe crisis in the marriage of a bereaved couple is the extramarital solace partners sometimes seek. Parents take this step into a fantasy life in order to escape into a world not crowded with their real-life tragedy.

One woman suffered dreadfully when her daughter died. She could not find a place for herself at home. She found her husband constantly hostile when she tried to talk about her grief. She would become infuriated, in turn, when he would grieve. They had no other children. Finally, in desperation, she got a job and wound up having an affair with a co-worker. To her, that relationship felt fresh and clean and unmarred by tragedy. At least that is how it seemed.

But, she confided, of all solutions in her need to escape, she had picked the worst one. She found herself not only saddled with her grieving and her husband's grieving, but now she had something brand-new to cause anguish—a guilty conscience.

Her pain became so great she sought counselling. She went alone at first until she had worked out the problem of her extramarital affair, which she ended. She did not wish to further agonize her husband by letting him know she had been unfaithful. When that was resolved, at least to the point where she could live with it, she insisted her husband come for help with her. He did, and the two, from what she says, have slowly begun to rebuild their life together. With a new start, something fresh and good has been allowed into their marriage.

Be kind to yourself. Do not set yourself up for further grief, further sorrow. You, of all people, do not need anything more to regret.

In fact, you need more things to bring pleasure back into your lives; things although small that lighten the burden and allow fresh air to enter a home stale from weeping. There is an old expression that originated in the deep south. It could well be a recipe for pleasure at this most important time for you:

"Do not let the seeds spoil your enjoyment of the watermelon; just spit them out!"

Although this is not easy to accept, to do, it is critical. There is absolutely no point in denying yourself some of the good things in life that can still be enjoyed as a couple—things like sex and socializing. Your enjoyment of these can only help ease the pain, and that is highly desirable.

You must believe relief is necessary because it is. You must not continue to exist together in a swamp, and until you are willing to allow some joy to enter your lives that is just what you are doing.

It is not uncommon for a wife to refuse sex because the idea of a pleasurable experience has become repugnant. One woman, now divorced, still cannot forgive her ex-husband for wanting to indulge in sex within a week after their daughter died.

"How could he outright seek sexual satisfaction with our little girl just dead?" the woman asks indignantly.

Her husband, tired of being made to feel like a lustful brute totally lacking in sensitivity, finally gave up trying to explain that for him sex was a release, a way of renewing himself.

"We reached an impasse that I am sure can never be breached," he said. "I know she will enjoy sex with another man, but not with the father of her dead child."

Another couple made it past this most sensitive and common

problem and are quite proud that it was done without outside help. Although they maintain that, had it been needed, they certainly would have sought a third party, they believe finding their own solution added another and positive dimension to their marriage.

After their child died of cancer, the woman simply froze. It was not a problem of enjoying a pleasurable experience. Instead, it went much deeper. In her mind, it was sex that originally brought their little boy into the world and by so doing exposed them to the agony they now suffered in their bereavement. She is quick to explain it was not a fear of pregnancy. She just did not want to go back to where it all began.

Her husband became more and more frustrated as weeks went by. Finally, in a burst of anger he told her they would either have sex together or he would have it with somebody else!

She saw he was not joking and it acted like a glass of cold water dashed into her face. The idea of her husband going outside their marriage for sex appalled her and she began to cry, saying she simply could not have relations with him because she would be unable to respond.

He held her in his arms and begged her to try. He said he knew their child was dead and he was horrified. But he was alive. He had needs. He told her they would try slowly to rebuild their shattered sex life. He would not expect her to respond at first. Just to be there. Maybe gradually one day her feeling would come back. He was convinced—and he succeeded in convincing her—that without participation there would be no hope of her feelings returning. It was a chance they had to take in order to save their marriage.

Somewhat fearfully, she went to bed with him and slowly in easy stages her responsiveness returned. She was able to wipe away the dreadful idea that sex should be denied because her son's death began with his conception.

Most couples are not that fortunate or well attuned to each other. Since sex is a basic drive, the problem of denying sex must be resolved. If you cannot work it out alone, seek counselling and do not delay.

Many couples have problems socializing after the death of a child. In most families one of the partners—not both—takes a "we must not enjoy ourselves" approach.

One young couple nearly lost that certain magic between them—a magic that is strong enough to be visibly evident— over the issue of socializing.

Their son had died at the age of four months following a bout with pneumonia. The husband, an appliance salesman, would go off to work in the morning leaving his wife to send their only other child, a four-year-old daughter, to nursery school. She then spent the rest of the day wandering their apartment, alone.

"My wife would be crying when I left and still crying when I came home," he said. "Well, I was sad too. But I still had a job to do, and when I got to work customers would come in and I ended up becoming absorbed and getting through the day one way or another.

"I would get home. There she would be, crying. It was like physically pulling me down every single day of the week. If I told her an amusing incident, she would look at me as if I were nuts for being able to go through a normal day.

"I began to dread coming home.

"One day, I decided this was going to stop. I was on the expressway, driving, and the idea of going home tied my stomach in knots. But I went anyhow and when I got there I insisted she get a sitter and we went to the movies. It was the first time we were out in three months. I made the mistake of laughing out loud at an amusing part of the cartoon and she jumped out of her seat, ran up the aisle, and waited for me in the lobby with tears streaming down her eyes."

The husband, obviously still uncomfortable at the remembrance, thumped one fist into his open hand when he told me the two stood there and argued in full voice in the theatre lobby.

"She started yelling at me and asking how I could be out in public laughing. Ricky was dead. What was wrong with me?"

"Well, I was embarrassed and furious. I am not sure which was worse. I loved that little kid too. I told her there was nothing wrong with laughing and going out. It meant no disrespect to our son's memory if we enjoyed ourselves. I also warned her I would leave unless she came to grips with this. I was scared when I said it but I meant it. I just could not go on the way we were."

As he related the incident, his wife sat there, her hand in his, tears running down her cheeks but with a small smile on her lips.

"He was absolutely right, you know. I had been giving in to my grief and not trying to handle it. I love him, and his threat to leave was the shock I needed to see where we were heading. I began to understand what harm I was doing to our marriage by not wanting or trying to do anything but grieve. Although we still have problems and I certainly still cry, I also know he cries too even if it is inward. I guess that is what I needed to be sure of. I can have fun with him now and not resent his enjoyment because I remember he cries inside too."

"Ricky has been dead a year, and since that flare-up our marriage has been stronger than ever."

Dealing, really dealing, with day-to-day problems is a special burden bereaved parents share—especially those whose child has died of a lingering illness. Generally, in such circumstances, all the normal everyday frustrations that one mate feels toward the other are rarely voiced.

It seemed ridiculous—and still does—that during a concentrated period of worry about our child trivia such as "Why don't you hang up your pants?" or "Why was dinner late again?" could even be discussed. Yet, this very absence of the airing of annoyances helped erode the foundation of our marriage. According to many psychiatric personnel, we were not unusual in this problem.

Ironically, we were warned that day-to-day living would present special problems because we had a dead child. We ignored those who cautioned us. We believed our union had been strong enough to fight for our child's life together, wait in hospital corridors together, attend his funeral together. Certainly it should be able to handle day-to-day problems easily enough.

We were wrong.

We made the great mistake of ignoring and overlooking—at least on the surface—ordinary irritants. Instead of discussing them and correcting them, anger-causing situations were allowed to accumulate.

What we were doing was shoving our problems under the rug. Just as hiding dirt under the carpet is bad housekeeping practice, doing the same with daily irritations is bad marriage practice. We were not wise enough to recognize the buildup of dirt and to seek help before we found ourselves with a mountain of rubbish.

We have now made a point of never allowing a recurrence of this buildup. We have a pact that any problem must be discussed within a day after it arises. If I am too angry to talk about something just as it happens, I will tell my husband, if he asks, that I am very put out indeed, but I need to cool down before I can talk.

Knowing I will keep my word allows him to take any pressure off me to discuss the issue at the moment of its hottest impact. Sometimes that daylong breather is essential in putting the matter into its proper perspective.

Just sharing a home demands perspective, too. It seems there are two sets of reactions to "home" for many bereaved fathers. Either they do not want to go out to work or they do not want to come home. They dread it.

One man, the owner of a carpet company, said his greatest battle in normalizing his life after his son died was the effort it took him to leave his house each morning.

"Somehow, it became my haven. The world seemed unfriendly and cold and uncaring. Leaving my house was my daily fight," he said.

His wife, a kind, sensitive, and practical woman, had created such a serene atmosphere despite her own grief, that her husband was really afraid to leave the cushioned aura of home. In order to help, she offered to go to his business with him on a part-time basis, thereby allowing him to take a part of "home" with him.

Gradually, he was able to make it alone.

Other fathers had the reverse problem. Their homes had become the symbol of death, pain, and mourning. A number of men said they used almost any excuse to stay late at the store or office. Others developed a new pattern—going out for a drink with the "boys" after work. Home to them meant hurt, not haven.

This response, of course, cannot help but create great animosity on the part of the wife. If they are not able to come to terms that are fair to both parties, this staying away from home will lead to gradual alienation and, frequently, to separation and divorce.

When a child dies, there are some people who change completely the patterns of their lives. They resort to younger looks, change jobs, change friends—in short, change everything. There are others who become more firmly entrenched in the patterns they have already established. One such woman had always been a good housekeeper. Windows washed, stove clean, refrigerator sparkling. Her home was neat but not uncomfortably so. Then her child died. She became so obsessed with cleaning that she would go into a rage if she discovered a fingerprint on the refrigerator. It was impossible to flick cigarette ashes twice into an ashtray without her jumping up to empty it.

As she leaned farther and farther to one extreme, her husband, who had never been great about doing household repairs, got worse. Washers were not replaced. Taps dripped. Windows needed caulking. While the wife was capable of making most of these repairs, she was extremely hostile because her husband refused to do them.

Plainly, the two were at loggerheads and heading for real difficulty. A friend, seeing how bad the situation had become, insisted they see a social worker, which they agreed to do.

The worker helped them reach a solution where their lives are now more comfortable. The wife has gotten a part-time job in the evenings. After taking care of her children, preparing dinner, and going off to work for three hours nightly, she no longer has the energy necessary to scrub already spotless counters. Everyone is more comfortable at home now.

As part of the agreement, her husband became the baby sitter while his wife worked. His job began with doing the dinner dishes and ended with getting the children off to bed. As the parent remaining at home, he too became annoyed with dripping taps and draughty windows. He had never really paid attention to them before. He began making the necessary repairs and developed a sense of pride in doing them.

This couple has found a positive future for their marriage

because an outsider was able to see the problems and their solutions far more easily than they themselves could have done.

While fathers with dead children have the difficult burden of still providing financially for their families even while they grieve, wives, too, have their own set of woes as they try to run their homes.

One of my most painful, hurtful, appalling experiences occurred the first time I went to the grocery after Robby died. I will never forget it. Every shelf, every aisle reminded me of my dead son. Either the item was something he hated or something he loved. Green beans and hot dogs and peanut butter sent stabs of pain through me.

After that first time, I became afraid to enter the grocery. I asked friends to pick up items such as milk for me. We ordered take-away food very often. My children eventually pushed me back to running a more normal home. They simply complained they were fed up with going to an empty refrigerator and pantry. They wanted food and meals and snacks. I felt so guilty that I asked a relative to go with me and, shaking, I did my marketing.

That second time, as in most steps toward coping with bereavement, was not as hard as my first shopping experience.

Interestingly, during this take-away period, my husband never exercised his right as my partner to object to the way I was running—or not running—the house. Because he understood how great my pain was, he made no demands on me and a situation was allowed to go on that should have been halted weeks before the children made it an issue.

Tolstoi once said, "The modern family is like a tiny little boat sailing in a storm on a vast ocean. It can keep afloat if it is ruled by one will. But when those in the boat begin struggling, the boat is upset."

This is probably especially true in the case of bereaved couples, with each member thrashing about trying to find his or her own solution for survival after the death of their child.

Sometimes the boat of family life is rocked its hardest over differing views of religion, even between parents of the same faith, when they are bereaved.

One couple, as an example, had become quite divided over the issue. He had turned away completely from religion. She had gone deper than ever into it. She attended mass daily and frequently prayed for her daughter's soul at home. She never outwardly mourned.

I was an uncomfortable observer to one of their quarrels over the issue.

"Now that Pammy is with God how can I be sad? It is the most glorious thing that can happen. I only thank Him for taking her so young, before she came to know the pain of this world," said the wife.

Her husband sat, squirming, as his wife expressed herself.

"Damn it," he yelled, "I am getting sick and tired of hearing how great it is that she is dead. It is not great. It stinks. She was beautiful. She was smart. She was my daughter and I will never be thankful she is dead. What is wrong with you?"

The mother arose with a superior and knowing smile on her face and simply left the room.

"This is what always happens," said the husband. "She gets up with a smart-aleck look on her face and leaves the room. How can she be grateful, *grateful*, Pammy is dead?"

I did not know how to respond to his anger or pain. One thing was evident, the two were working at cross-purposes while trying to achieve a common goal—some peace. It was also evident the pair needed to let some fresh air into their relationship in order to create open-mindedness.

Eventually, and by much good fortune, the parish priest

came to visit the couple. He had never before met the husband. An intuitive man, he saw how they pulled at each other and the ugly antagonism that resulted.

He invited the husband to visit him in the parish office just to talk—"no strings attached." The husband, seeing the priest was not one to strew every sentence with "God will provide" and "God will make everything all right," responded.

The man told me he and the priest have become friendly. Although the husband will never be as religious as his wife, he no longer tries to undermine her main source of comfort. The wife, too, has mellowed. The priest has cautioned her about using God as an abrasive force rather than a healing one.

Some bereaved couples have managed to retain viable marriages by herding together for the common good. It is by far the simplest and possibly the best solution for all but the most gut-level problems. One such group of parents is active in the Michigan Leukemia Foundation.

Mrs. Sylvia Brown, executive director of the organization, said her group defies the negative statistics generally applied to bereaved parents. Since the foundation was formed in 1952, she claims that, of the one hundred fifty couples actively working to combat the blood disease which had taken their child, only one had divorced.

Mrs. Brown said when couples come to the foundation, attend the meetings, and become involved, they seem to do well with each other.

This common interest, fighting the dread killer, may well serve to keep communication lines open, thereby eliminating the possibility of an insidious alienation.

Although the dynamics of a situation change, I do think our own marriage could have been helped considerably had we become active in an organization for bereaved parents. I believe this not only because of the experience of couples active in the Leukemia Foundation but because of a recent experience of my own.

I am certain it would be wrong to make a cult of death. But while researching for this book, I discovered a truth when I attended my first meeting for bereaved parents. This was one of a number of organizations designed to help people who had suffered a loss such as ours. In all the years since the time of my son's death, I have never felt more comfortable and at home than at that meeting.

First off, I did not need to decide whether to tell the people around me of my irretrievable loss. This is a common problem bereaved people face when socializing or any time they meet someone new. For years after Robby died, when a stranger would ask how many children we had, I was frankly stuck for an answer. Every bereaved couple I know has been faced with this dilemma.

Secondly, and most important, I heard people discussing problems that had arisen from and during their bereavement that we too had experienced. These people sat in a group atmosphere, a friendly one, and talked about situations and arrived at solutions that for us, in our aloneness, had been festering sores lacking the air needed to heal.

The thing I heard that first time was a frank and open discussion by people who were travelling the same muddy road we had travelled. To a bereaved parent, there can be no one more believable than someone who has been there and knows where the potholes really lie.

It can be of enormous benefit for you, as bereaved parents, to involve yourselves in some organization of this sort. If your children are old enough, by all means include them.

As a bereaved parent-mate, there are certain positive steps that you can take—indeed, you must take. You have already lost enough without forfeiting your marriage. Use reason, not vindictiveness. Remember, you loved your spouse enough to marry. Be gentle and do not blame your mate for what you were powerless to prevent—your child's death. For many couples, joining in some mutually agreeable social-betterment project has filled at least in part that void created by the death of a child. The project need not necessarily be related to the problem that caused your child's death. There are many community service organizations that need volunteers. Try to find one together. A joint interest in something can be very gratifying and can open new vistas in your relationship.

Do not presume you have all the answers to solving marital problems when you have a dead child. Normally it is hard enough to be objective. Nearly all your vision can leave after undergoing such a tragedy. You cannot evaluate a problem clearly when you cannot see.

Be kind enough to yourselves to recognize you badly need a third party to talk with even if you do not recognize stress in your relationship. It is there. Most cities have social service agencies with qualified people who will listen. Along with the major disease-oriented organizations such as the Heart, Kidney Disease and Cancer groups, there are any number of helping places available at little or no cost. Most communities list their social service departments in the telephone directory. Help can also be gotten by calling most psychiatric departments in hospitals—particularly children's hospitals. Your church or synagogue can also assist you in finding people who will help. Your local newspaper can sometimes help locate such groups. Many areas have information centres that can direct you to someone or someplace for help. Frequently the National Association for Mental Health can guide you*

While some places can help more effectively than others, you will have made a positive beginning.

Do not forget that life goes on and with it come day-to-day

* In Britain, bereavement counselling is available under many Local Authorities; and The Compassionate Friends is a nation-wide self-help organisation of bereaved parents. Check for a local group—or help form one.

problems. Do not sweep them under the rug. Do not fear your mate's anger. Tell him to stop avoiding coming home at night. Tell her you expect dinner to be prepared. If you do not take these basic concrete steps you will find yourself walking on separate sides of the river of grief with no bridge upon which to meet.

Above all and beyond all, remember everyone must carry his own mourning. It is something that cannot be shared. Do not make demands of comfort from your mate when he is feeling the same pain you feel. Recognize that she would help if she could. You must content yourself with this if you wish your marriage to survive.

Value that marriage. You have lost enough.

*Oh call my brother back to me! I
cannot play alone; The summer comes
with flower and bee—where is my
brother gone?*

—FELICIA DOROTHEA HEMENS

BEREAVEMENT AND SIBLINGS

One of the most difficult roles for a mother or father, when a child dies, is to continue being a parent to surviving offspring.

Suddenly, such a parent is thrust into a role almost beyond what may reasonably be expected of a human being. Parenthood now takes on the dimension of helping a youngster faced with the enormity of adjusting to the death of a person of his own generation. It means groping to find the right words and attitudes to comfort a living brother or sister. It means helping fill the void left by the dead child who formerly shared a table, games, a bedroom, the same preferences in television programmes. And the emptiness of not having that person to share with can be unfathomable.

Mothering and fathering means nursing a child, spiritually, back to health after a part has been severed.

Parenthood now becomes walking and talking and listening and hearing someone else at a time when it takes everything just to think or function for oneself.

Unfortunately, many surviving children suffer because their parents were unable to fulfill this responsibility, and the effects of their inability can be lifelong.

When Robby died, our instinctive thought was to get home and be with our children who had been left in the care of family. Friends at home badgered an airline until we got emergency seats on an already full airplane because we felt our children needed us.

We were right. They did. But six years later, our son, who was twelve when his brother died, remembers feeling unloved and alone during the entire grieving period and indeed for several years thereafter.

In discussing this with surviving siblings, many of whom are now middle-aged, a recurrent theme appears to be that the living children received precious little by way of comfort from their parents.

"I kept looking for some help from my mother after my brother died," said a woman in her late forties. "Although he died when I was sixteen, I'll never forget that feeling of aloneness—or how frightened I was because neither my mother nor father seemed reachable. I really don't remember them trying very hard to help me. They were too busy with their own grief."

The woman, now married and a parent, made her statement without condemnation because a quarter century had elapsed since her brother's death.

"I was angry with them because they made me feel I was being shoved aside just when I needed them the most. I see now they were incapable of giving me any more than they did," she said.

"Years later, my mother and I discussed that terrible time and it was kind of funny. She could only recall what a maximum effort she exerted to try to console me. She claimed it was the only effort she was able to put forth for anyone. Her recollections may be true, but if she did reach out and try to help me, she obviously did not succeed because I only remember being very alone."

This woman was not alone in feeling a sense of parental abandonment at this terrible and crucial time. In a three-person interview conducted with teen-agers, my son, nineteen, and two girls, sixteen and eighteen, said substantially the same thing in recalling just what happened when their brothers and sisters died.

We discussed the emotional upheaval created by a dead sibling. The answers I received saddened me because I would dearly have profited from them at the time they were most pertinent. Also, it showed me how short of the mark my husband and I fell despite thinking at the time we had handled things well.

The three used such words as "disgusting," "unreal," and "phoney" to describe their dead siblings' funerals.

"It went on forever," said Carol, sixteen. Her twenty-five-year-old married sister, with whom she was very close, has been dead four years.

"I wanted to be alone with my mother instead of in a family room filled with crying relatives," said Diane, eighteen, and now an only child whose fifteen-year-old brother died two years ago. Her father had died six months before that.

"The whole funeral was just to see a bunch of people make a buck and it was phoney," said my son.

And he reiterated what Diane said:

"I wanted to be quiet and be with my parents and my sister; instead, there were so many people."

The grieving process for a surviving brother or sister is, in many ways, like that of a parent, but there are differences. The three teen-agers who come from widely divergent backgrounds showed a surprising degree of similarity in this process.

"I never slept at home, and all I wanted to do was run, run, and run from my mother because after the funeral all she did was cry. I always ended up comforting her instead of her comforting me. I still dislike her for it," said Diane.

"I was gone a lot of the time," echoed Carol. "No one seemed to care about me. Suddenly there were no rules and no strictness in my home. It was the first time I saw my father cry. I felt very frightened and very alone. My mother was practically incoherent and worse than useless. She seemed to want comfort from me when it was my sister, my older sister whom I could always talk to, who was dead."

My son agreed with some of these sentiments and added a few comments of his own about the period of grieving.

"I felt like I had been pushed aside and I used to cry in my bedroom. I wanted to be talked to as a person, but instead I felt like a burden every time I tried to speak to you and Dad about Robby. The thing I wanted most was my parents' time so we could talk, but that rarely happened. Instead, our house seemed like it was always filled with people."

One emotion generally felt by a bereaved parent was not experienced by the three young people. None of them underwent the awful feeling of powerlessness to save the dead that most parents endured. Their load of pain was great enough without that, however, when they discussed guilt.

And of course, in nearly all cases, such guilt is unfounded. Despite a normal and healthy share of arguing with Robby, who was three years his junior, Dale was a most considerate brother. Like any boy reaching Little League age, Robby badly wanted to play on a ball team and wear a Little League uniform. When his cardiologist told him baseball was out of the question, Robby was faced with one of the saddest days of a young life already filled with too many hospital stays and too much illness.

It was his brother with his innate kindness who helped ease Robby's disappointment.

A ball player of no small ability and already playing on a Little League team, he convinced his coach to allow Robby to be the team's batboy. When he came home and told Robby that a baseball team job—and one that included a uniform—was his for the taking, the joy in his brother's face should have lasted Dale for all time.

But it didn't. He didn't even remember this or any number of similar acts of kindness. He forgot completely how he always brought Robby candy from parties. How he stayed home sometimes and played nonaction games with his brother instead of running off with boyfriends. How he used to ride him on his bicycle on days when Robby was too tired to pedal his own.

Instead, he remembered only arguing and bad feeling. And worse yet, his recollections made the disagreements appear larger than they had actually been.

"I used to have nightmares that he died because I punched him," said my son. "It took me years to understand that I had nothing to do with his death."

Carol's guilt took on an entirely different form. She felt God had dealt this terrible blow because she was jealous of the attention her dead sister had given her own children. That attention and affection had once been Carol's.

"I used to go over there and see her playing with the babies —they were two and three—and she suddenly had no time to talk with me. It seemed like I was being shut out of her life. I would go home sometimes hating the babies because I wanted all my sister's attention. Then she developed cancer and died. I never told anyone but I always felt God had punished me because of my jealousy. There was just no one I could tell."

Diane had her own set of woes. She and her brother had been very close until the year of his death in an automobile accident.

"Things started to go bad that year between us. We were only a year apart in age and we used to do everything together. Then my father got sick and died. My brother seemed to go into a shell and he excluded me. I was very hurt because we had always shared feelings as well as fun.

"The farther he went into his shell, the more I decided to ignore him. If he couldn't communicate with me, well, I just would not pay attention to him. In the space of six months we grew to be almost strangers. And then came the car accident and he died. I never had a chance to patch things up and now I never will."

The three were of different faiths but, sadly, their views of organized religion were completely shared; none of them wanted anything to do with it although their parents practiced some form of worship.

"If there is a God how could he let my brother die?" asked my son.

Carol, while still believing in God, said she would hesitate to put her trust in Him if someone else she loved were near death.

Diane said since the two deaths there is very little religion in her home.

"I am glad about that, too. After all, what is praying? When my brother was in the intensive care unit after the accident I prayed and prayed for God to spare him. It's not good enough to be told we will meet in an afterlife. I need him now. Praying is just mouthing a bunch of words."

The three said that a great deal of the explanation by their parents of their siblings' deaths was God-related.

"It was God's will" and "Now he belongs to God" was the general tone set in all three homes.

It evidently was a mistaken method of handling.

All were left with no one to ask for help at a time that such aid could have helped them immeasurably. They agreed that, properly exercised, religion might still have remained a part of their lives. But, strangely, all three sets of parents somehow gave the impression, however inadvertent, that God had made a bad decision and was therefore to blame for the tragedy. Or else, God was persecuting their family.

The three also felt death touched every phase of their lives. In the time after the tragedies, home represented sadness rather than sanctuary. Nothing in their houses, it seemed to them, had any positive meaning and so they were gone a great deal of the time.

"I always went out to my friends' houses," said Carol. "I would go hoping to have fun and above all to get away from the atmosphere at home, the sadness and emptiness. My parents were always angry because I was constantly making plans to stay overnight or have dinner at some friend's house. I couldn't explain to them just how much our house meant death to me and nothing more."

Diane's efforts to find some pleasure in life were frowned upon by any number of well-meaning aunts and uncles.

"I hated our house, but they would come over and say, 'Be with your mother. Try to help her.' They just never understood. I didn't have enough strength to help her. I needed all my energy just to go to school. There is one aunt I no longer speak to at all. She came over one Sunday and began yelling about my going out all the time. She finally said, 'Don't you think of your brother at all?' I told her to go to hell and I left the house. We have never said a word to one another since that day."

The three share another common factor—their dislike of visiting their siblings' graves.

"I wouldn't go unless I was dragged." Carol.

"You get there and it's nothing." Diane.

"Going serves no purpose other than making me sick." Dale.

Carol has not gone to the cemetery since her brother's death.

"Sometimes, I think about going but I never do, and if I did, it would be by myself. Not with my parents. I resent their insistence that I go. Their loss is not my loss. By the same token my loss is not theirs. If and when I visit my sister's grave it will be by myself. It will be a very individual and personal thing for me. I'll be there someday. Not yet, though. And certainly not because my parents badger me about it."

The sadness I felt as a parent and interviewer was very great at the end of this session. In six years as a member of a bereaved family, this was the first time my son had ever expressed how he really felt about Robby's death and its effect upon him, despite having open discussions on nearly every imaginable subject.

In a sense I am luckier than the other two mothers. They still do not know what their children's thoughts were and are. This is another tragedy when a child dies. Somehow, and I suspect it's true in nearly all families, there is no depth of communication about feelings surrounding the dead sibling. It would be a rare child that could face his tear-stained bereaved mother and tell her "I hated my brother sometimes. I even used to wish he was dead. Is that why he died?" Yet this sentiment is often felt by a youngster who has been tattled upon, beaten up, or just infuriated by a sister or brother.

Certainly, of course, there must be children who emerged from this tragedy with less anger and more of a feeling of being understood, but social workers say that generally children who survive the death of a brother or sister find a focal point for their anger. Frequently, that focus is their "mistreatment" by authoritarian figures like parents, relatives, teachers, and even God.

Perhaps the real lesson children learn from having a brother or sister die is that not everything in life is fair or good. Some things are tragic. There is no getting around that. It is one of those things that cannot come out all right. To be young and faced with the magnitude of that truth can be awesome.

Children who from infancy turned instinctively to their parents to ease hurts suddenly and in the worst possible light see another side of a mother or father. They see their parents in roles of impotence. They see them overwhelmed by death and they too are overwhelmed. They expect solace from people who themselves need consoling.

Another problem siblings sometimes face is the almost inevitable comparison with the dead child. In most households there is a natural rivalry between brothers and sisters whether for parents' attention, school grades, or winning at games. Parents, depending on the circumstances, favour one child at a given moment and another child at a different time. This goes on in all homes and is a maturing phenomenon.

When a child dies, parents have an obligation to the surviving siblings; they must see to it that once healthy sibling rivalry does not become an unwholesome memory or emotion.

A suburban elementary school teacher told me of an instance where she had in her tutor group a bright and popular boy who died of leukaemia in the middle of a school year.

"Brian was delightful. Just delightful. He was an outstanding math student. Was the class president. And, above all, had a marvellous sense of humour. I remember him now and I still feel like smiling even though I am saddened by his death."

The teacher said Brian had a brother, just a year younger, who apparently was destined to follow in his popular brother's footsteps.

"When Brian died, Craig's fourth-grade teacher told me that much of Brian's pleasantness and scholastic aptitude was also present in his brother. I remember thinking what a consolation this would be for their parents.

"By the time Craig reached my class the following year, any likeness to Brian was undetectable. Craig was a surly, aggressive boy who obviously exerted no effort in his studies. The situation deteriorated to the point where Craig was becoming a bully, and finally, reluctantly, I called his mother to school.

"She came into my room and there was that same niceness about her I had seen in Brian. When I explained the problem she told me she had noticed the change at home and just couldn't understand it. She said she and her husband had any number of times spoken with Craig. They had even told him he had something worthwhile to live up to—Brian's memory."

The teacher said that, as Craig's mother continued to tell of how his problems were handled at home, the reason for his behaviour became quite evident. Craig could think of only one way to escape an impossible rivalry with a dead brother. He would not compete. He would be as different as possible. The similarity between them created comparison, and in that comparison the living child paled before the memory of the dead.

"I recommended counselling and took the plunge by telling the mother forthrightly how I viewed the problem. She was shocked. At first, she seemed to reject what I had said. Then she agreed. By the end of that school year, the surly class bully could laugh and play well again. There were times, though, when I caught a faraway look in his eye, and a certain sadness would overtake him. I am sure these were the times he thought of his dead brother and missed him."

There are, of course, no limits to the individual problems parents and siblings face when trying to cope with a child's death. Even as adults, very few people have completely worked through their philosophy of not existing any longer. Because of this, there is always a certain awkwardness in trying to help another human being through the enormity of an immediate family death.

If a parent has unresolved feelings about death, whether they be fear, uncertainty about an afterlife, or just a negative view generally, these feelings cannot help being transmitted to children—especially young children. Psychiatrists generally agree that very little by way of an explanation is helpful to a child under four years of age because the concept is just too enormous to be grasped by one with so limited a life experience.

I found this particularly true when trying to explain Robby's death to our extremely intelligent four-year-old daughter.

I tried, initially, to be truthful and wound up with a lie which is, of course, contrary to most psychiatric and personal principles. When we returned from Alabama, our house was in a state of uproar. There was no place not occupied by well-meaning friends and family. Our rabbi had told Dale the tragic news, but the task of explaining to Stacie why she would never again see her beloved brother was left to us.

It was dark when we returned home. My daughter and I sat looking out at the stars from our front window and talked. That conversation, one of my life's hardest, is etched indelibly in my mind.

I began by simply saying Robby was dead. She asked, "For how long will he be dead?" I replied, "Forever. He will never be back." But a four-year-old, no matter how astute, just cannot grasp "forever." I could see how puzzled and frightened she was.

She asked what happens when a person dies. And here I used

extreme care, consciously avoiding the dangerous pitfall of saying "he went to sleep." I believe such a statement could induce a fear of sleep that could last forever. Instead, I said he stopped breathing. I heard her take a deep breath and try to hold it. She said she couldn't do that too long. I agreed, and said it was because she was a healthy child.

Up to the point of the inevitable "Why?" things went well. I answered as simply and honestly as her four-year-old level and my personal horror permitted.

Then came the toughie.

"Why?"

I began by saying he was very sick and she countered with she had been sick many times. I said Robby was a different kind of sick.

"Robby was good. He played with me. He'll be scared not to be home. Why did he die?"

Again I responded with "He was very sick." Although I used the phrase repeatedly, it held absolutely no meaning for her. My answer just was not penetrating. This was evident. She could only relate his never coming home again to how fearful she would feel if that happened to her.

Finally, perhaps more out of desperation than judgment, I told her he had been in a great deal of pain and we must be grateful he no longer was hurting.

Although it was not true, it had at least the virtue of being tangible. Something she could understand. After all, hurt was a bad thing and she did not wish this for her brother.

After that, the "why" stopped.

Whether or not telling a lie is always wrong, I will leave up to psychiatrists and moralists. I only knew she desperately needed something. Some explanation. I offered her one that she was able to grasp. When she was ten I told her I had lied. At first she was angry. But when I explained why I had done it, she told me she understood. Normally I deal truthfully with my children and she knows that. She has said since she was grateful for an explanation that at least "made sense."

At a seminar for social workers, psychologists categorized what they considered the proper information to be given a child according to the youngster's age.

They maintained children of five, at the earliest, can understand death is final. Generally by that time they have seen dead small animals and the like. They caution that if the child wants to know the time, don't build him a watch. Tell the truth simply and with a minimum of elaboration unless questions are asked. Whether or not you wish to include God in your explanation is an individual thing. Remember, though, not to make Him appear a culprit to be hated at some later time in your child's life.

They claim children of six have been found to be generally quite emotional about death, so the need to tread lightly is great. Be gentle and try not to invoke fear by allowing your own fears to come through.

A child of seven, especially in this television-oriented society where even cartoon characters die, is at a stage of curiosity about death although not yet ready to face up to it. By the age of eight, a youngster is more sophisticated, and, from that age on, explanations can be on a more mature level.

Psychologists at the seminar stressed the importance of knowing your own child and using the age breakdowns merely as guidelines.

To allow very young children to attend the funeral of a dead brother or sister is an individual judgment. As a rule of thumb, nothing constructive can be gained by taking a child under seven to such a tragic rite. Psychiatrists, for the most part, agree with this. Yet, from time to time, our daughter will express anger because she did not attend her brother's funeral.

Even to this day, we are told "He was my brother and I should have been there."

When I tell her she was much too young, she always replies she was not too young to know he was not home. In our family, at least, the right or wrong of the decision to keep her home from the funeral will never be fully resolved.

William Cowper said, "Knowledge is proud that it knows so much; wisdom is humble it knows no more." This principle becomes most pronounced when trying to guide children through the tricky quicksand of grief. All the knowledge we had about Robby's illness and about trying to help our children through the ordeal of bereavement did not give us enough wisdom to help them through the trying time after he died. Dale should not have been allowed to feel alone. Stacie probably should have attended the funeral. We were not capable of foresight because we were blinded with sorrow.

In later years, some of the difficulties can be remedied, but not entirely corrected, by the parents. It takes great energy, effort, and striving for companionship to fill the void created by a dead child. But it is a goal worth groping toward.

At the time a child dies, surviving children must become the uppermost concern—almost beyond a parent's own grief Properly handled or rectified soon enough, this concern can mean the continuation of the family as a companionable unit. It requires an enormous strength to deal with others' hurts at such a time, but it is important not to allow a living child to feel alone. Use any reserve you have to take time through the initial grieving process to switch roles from the comforted to the comforter. That means sitting and talking with your child quietly or reading or listening together to a record. The need for your individual attention is great.

Do not allow a breakdown of discipline in your home. Discipline and order mean security to a child. Don't pull the rug out from under him or her during this, the worst possible time.

Allow this discipline, however, to be of a calm, relaxed variety. Heavy-handedness is rarely good handling. It is even less so in this situation. Instead, allow good sense to be the order of the day. This is not easy when faced with an insensible situation, but in working to salvage what is left of your family it is imperative.

In taking time to talk separately with each living child, ask enough questions to help reveal *then* any feelings of guilt that could be harbored by your youngster for years.

Remind the child of the good acts—and there always are some good acts—performed for the dead sibling.

Explain that a reasonable amount of quarrelling is normal between brothers and sisters.

Explain to a child aged seven or older that wishing a person dead, a very natural thought when angered, does not create a dead person.

Tread carefully about religion if you wish your child to remain observant. "God's will" is less than consolation to a youngster who sees a brother's roller skates sitting in the closet never to be worn again.

Do not condemn children for laughing and playing during the early stages of bereavement. No living person, regardless of age, can handle healthily such grief in one lump.

Do not push children to go to the cemetery. Let them take the lead. Some adults need more time to work things through than do others. The same applies to children.

Do not turn your normal good-bad child into a saint just because he is dead. No one can compete with a ghost—especially one who no longer possesses any bad qualities. Living children may react opposite to all the "goodness" in order to gain attention.

Remember, your children are suffering just as you are suffering. They also fear the strength of their grief.

Try to explain as naturally as possible that there is a lot we don't understand about death, and repeatedly emphasize that death is beyond anyone's control.

Do not avoid talking about your dead child. He or she existed. Let surviving children remember that.

Not all life is happy and, unfortunately for bereaved siblings, they will carry a certain sadness with them for all time. Let them at least have an honest memory to hold.

Above all, it is not necessary to hide your own grief. Encourageing a child to air his sorrow can be the greatest gift—other than your time—that you can give. Remind him, though, you share a loss that, although not identical, is at least mutual.

For many children, the early stages of bereavement will be the first time youngsters will see their father cry. And certainly the father should cry. Handled with care this does not have to create panic in children.

One father said he was startled at the look of fear in his eleven-year-old son's eyes when the boy saw him crying.

"He may have other bad feelings about his sister's death, but he did learn one thing from that time. He learned men feel pain and cry.

"When I saw how afraid he was, I took him into his bedroom and put my arms around him and explained how sad I felt about his sister's death. I told him crying is not just for girls and mothers. Boys and fathers also have the right to show how bad they feel.

"We sat there, then, the two of us and cried with our arms around each other."

This was a lucky father in one sense. His son did not get lost in a crowd of well-wishers.

In retrospect, most of my son's feelings of being left to his own devices stemmed from our being so surrounded with concerned adults. Our family would have fared better as a unit had we appointed someone to act as a buffer for us and to explain we needed some time—even half an hour—to be alone together. Many misconceptions could have been worked through then and there had we known that we should spend some time with our children.

Perhaps the greatest and saddest lesson I learned from interviewing teen-agers and men and women who endured the death of siblings in their childhood, is that no one remembered a positive interplay with parents during the grieving period. Prod as I would and question as I did, I was unable to come up with any situation in which parents had been able to put aside their own mourning to comfort these children.

Certainly this book has not been written to cast blame. It is the last thing I intend. Instead, we should all take this lesson carefully to heart and examine our dealings during the grieving period. It is not too late to undo some of the mistakes we have made.

If explanations were muddled, feelings hurt, sorrow ignored, tears left unshed, by all means open the subject again and honestly discuss what mistakes in handling have been made.

Any number of families with whom I spoke viewed this as the hardest hurdle in coping with grieving.

"I hate to bring it up," said one mother.

"After all, the kids are going about their business—why make them cry or unhappy?" agreed a father.

"I don't know what to say," said another mother. "We have never talked about it."

Well, perhaps it's about time it was talked about. That is the beauty of dealing with surviving children. It need not be too late.

There's only one thing worse than
speaking ill of the dead—and that is
not speaking of the dead at all.

—ANONYMOUS

BEREAVEMENT
AND
COMMUNICATING

One of the difficult truths for the nonbereaved parent to accept is that a dead child not only should but must be discussed.

The most essential ingredient, in fact, in surviving well—besides facing reality—is to speak of the dead child unashamedly.

With the exception of one woman, who found our speaking freely of Robby very awkward, most people whose friendship we have retained said it eased a problem for them too.

"After all," said one friend, "it's such a hard thing that you just don't know what to do. As someone close to Robby and you, I myself felt the need to talk with you about him. It was a relief to see I would not have to always guard myself about the subject."

Another aspect of this difficult social problem became apparent when we realized nearly everyone we knew had children Robby's age.

I remember almost gritting my teeth before asking one acquaintance or another how their little boy or girl was doing in school or on a ball team. It was one of those hurdles that I felt had to be overcome in order to retain normalcy in any relationship that mattered to me.

Another friend still remembers what a help it was that I took the initiative and asked about other people's children.

"The whole question of my own kids was almost embarrassing," he said. "Here I was the father of a healthy boy just starting on a bowling team. I was afraid, when we saw you, that I would burst out about how well he was doing. After all, I didn't want to make you feel worse by rubbing your nose in my child's progress. It was a great relief to me when you asked us, in the restaurant one Saturday night, how Kenny was doing. It seemed to free something in our relationship."

Surprisingly, I still remember asking the question because our two boys had been rather friendly. I recall what a conscious effort it took to appear interested when I really wasn't at the time. Actually, the only reason I asked was to accomplish what it obviously did. I put a dear friend at his ease and removed a barrier that could have divided a close relationship.

It seems impossible to me to understand the cruelty of friends and family who desert parents at such a time. But in my research I found countless couples who had horror stories to relate, such as a brother, once close, who stopped calling his sister shortly after her child died, or friends who were never heard from again after the funeral.

As bad as the problem is for parents whose children died of normal diseases such as cancer or heart difficulties, the social morass of the mother or father whose offspring has killed himself is almost beyond any imaginable depth.

These people suffer not only guilt and loneliness; they all too often suffer from ostracism.

"One of the worst things that ever happened since Alan shot himself," said one father, who has since begun drinking very heavily, "is the way my former friends cannot look me in the eye. It's as if one of us is harbouring a guilty secret that we cannot share. I sometimes almost get the feeling these people look at us as if we were murderers. My wife and I don't like to see them anymore. It hurts too much."

Perhaps the beginnings of this type of alienation lie in the awkwardness of not knowing what to say. This discomfort can create a million excuses for a friend or relative not to call a bereaved parent. One day falls hard upon another, and suddenly the friend looks around and a month has gone by without making that difficult phone call. Now, with the time lapse, along with the awkwardness comes the need for apology, and once again the evasion "too busy" to make that call takes hold. Soon, enough time has elapsed to make the problem so embarrassing that it's simply easier to forget the whole thing.

I believe, after much investigation, that, unfair as it may seem, the burden for sustaining relationships rests with the bereaved parents. At a time when it is most difficult to do, they are placed in the position of having to take the initiative of making that first call, extending that first invitation.

Let me urge you, also, while making that call, not to wreck the entire mood of conciliation by peevishness.

"How come you haven't called?"

"Where have you been?"

"What could be new after my tragedy?"

It would not be unnatural to think these sentiments, but to voice them? I would suggest not. You may end up with just someone upon whom you vented anger, rather than a friend.

Instead, strike a tone of friendship. Extend a friendly hand.

People do want to help. They just need to be shown how.

Any number of people have told me parents ultimately benefit who are willing to make the first move, either in talking about their child, asking about someone else's, or dialling the phone. By taking that first step, the danger is averted of the awkward pause that could last a lifetime.

Psychiatrist Elliot Luby said he cannot emphasize strongly enough the need for people to stand by bereaved parents and yet, in his experience, most couples are abandoned.

"That is almost the worst part of the whole problem," he said. "In the grieving process, everything depends on the sources of support. When people are there, compassionate and accepting people, it sometimes can reduce the intensity of grief."

Speaking about a dead child can sometimes lead to the strangest conversations. Not long ago, I visited a woman whose fifty-five-year-old son had died of a coronary. He was married and the father of three children. As it happens, we knew her son well.

During the course of the visit, the woman began talking about someone and described his virtues. She said he never gambled, never drank, and was the only man she knew who never swore.

Not being in the room when the conversation began, it took me several minutes to realize she was speaking of her son, our dead friend. She had managed to make a deity of a perfectly normal decent sort of guy who was a good friend, mixed a great cocktail, and could tell a good off-colour story.

I didn't argue with the woman. There was no point. But I felt somehow that Len's mother was doubly cheated. Not only was her son dead. She no longer knew him as he was.

By not remembering the real, living man, his mother could

not pay him the greatest respect of all—that of truthful re-membrance.

Early after Robby's death, just as we had made a pact to talk about him, my husband and I also agreed to try to re-member him as he was. Somehow, without knowing quite why, it seemed right.

Our son was sometimes good, sometimes bad, sometimes willful, and sometimes loving. He was real. Because we did not haze our memory or distort it, I think that, these years later, we are left with something more tangible—the memory of a real person—than are parents who totally renovate their child's character after death.

Another step in maintaining relationships by properly com-municating is to admit you need help and comfort. One mother, a very kind and compassionate elderly lady, often went to funerals for close friends and offered to help bereaved relations in any way she could.

"I would tell people all they had to do was call. I would be there for them. I could never understand it but the calls just did not come. About a year ago, I telephoned a widowed friend and asked how things were going. She said things were fine and, even though I did not believe her, I felt I could push her no farther.

"My son died recently after a long siege of cancer. When people first called, I replied with the same trite answer my friends used when asked how things were. I would say every-thing is just great. Wonderful, in fact.

"I realized something was wrong when people gradually stopped calling. Then, it came to me. I was falling into the same trap and setting up the same roadblocks with people that my own friends had created with me.

"The next time a friend called, I gritted my teeth and told

the truth. I said I felt terrible. It was awful to know my son would never telephone or visit again. I levelled with the woman and told her I needed her help and companionship. I asked her to please come to dinner.

"My friend thanked me for telling her how I felt and said she was grateful I had told her how to help. I have never fallen into that 'feeling wonderful' trap again."

Perhaps the fundamental lesson in this is that people are basically decent. My experience has shown they truly want to help. After all, it is most difficult to live with oneself knowing you have deserted a bereaved family.

But, as in many human endeavours, people need guidance. They need to be shown how. The responsibility for maintaining social relationships often comes to rest with the bereaved. We are the ones who must set the tone and pace for social relationships. If we don't, we may find that no one will.

Contact your friends. Ask how family members are. Put people at their ease by speaking freely. Don't be dishonest and play "feeling wonderful" when you don't mean it. Invite someone over for coffee. Or, suggest meeting at a restaurant for a meal. Sometimes being in a public place can help you gain control of your emotions, thereby making a more pleasurable social contact. Don't forget to maintain a sense of balance.

You should not be maudlin; neither do you have to be merry. Be you, but with this added insight: consider their well-intentioned awkwardness.

I remember the first time we were invited to a close friend's for dinner just after Robby died. When we went into the dining room and sat down it suddenly occurred to all of us that an extra place had been set.

My friend, who had stood by us throughout the ordeal, had mechanically arranged the table for the same number of people as before.

We all saw that place setting at the same time. I took the dishes off, teased my hostess about not being able to count, and made light of a small but horrible episode. By my doing so, she was able to brush aside a tear and go on serving her kind and thoughtful meal.

It is entirely possible—if not probable—that your first act of initiative may fail. In fact, you may fall flat on your face. But the second time you take the initiative will be easier until eventually you have mastered the art of communicating although bereaved.

*Most people have some sort of religion
—at least they know which church
they're staying away from.*

—JOHN ERSKINE

BEREAVEMENT
AND
RELIGION

Of all the confusing emotions to which a bereaved parent is subjected, perhaps the most difficult is that stemming from one's attitude toward religion.

Many families, after a child dies, seem to turn entirely toward an organized religious belief as an anchor—something to hold onto or something that will hold onto them.

For many people, regardless of their faith, a belief that there was a divine purpose in their child's death is just what they need to sustain them. They can be comfortable thinking the death was not just an empty, meaningless happening. They feel God had a greater plan and their beloved Jimmy or Janie was a part of that plan.

I believe such people are very fortunate. They are relieved of a sense of the futility of things.

People who are religious are the ones who can ask "Why did this happen to me," without destroying themselves emotionally. They can give themselves many answers.

One ancient example of this is the tale of the wife of a revered and wise rabbi whose twin sons died while he was away from home.

Knowing how deeply he loved the boys, his wife decided to keep the tragic news from her husband until he could fortify himself with dinner that evening. When the rabbi came home, he asked for his sons repeatedly. His wife always replied, "They are away from home now."

After the meal, she sat with him and said, "You are a very wise and learned man. Help me with the answer to a problem. If you were lent two precious jewels and told you could enjoy them as long as they were in your keeping, would you be able to argue when the lender asked for their return?"

Her husband thought for a moment and replied, "Certainly not!"

His wife then arose and led her husband into the bedroom where the two boys lay, dead, and said, "God wanted his jewels back."

The most fortunate people are those who can derive peace from thinking their child is with God. They are the parents who do not constantly rack themselves with the pain of thinking how useless it was that their child died. And even if they do ask why, they have an answer that will not satisfy those who are nonbelievers.

Although no numbers are available to determine if larger numbers of bereaved parents turn to or away from religion, there is no question that many couples belong to the latter group.

Why? Perhaps from bitterness or disillusionment. Or, in the case of lingering illness, because God did not answer the parents' prayers. Some formerly deeply religious people have turned away because they believe He didn't listen to their pleadings.

Many bereaved parents take just such an approach—a sense of betrayal by God. They went many places for help when their child was sick. They sought doctors and hospitals and found people responded and usually with the best effort they could give. Then, at the ultimate moment, they turned to God for help but he did not respond. Now, in their sorrow, they will not allow themselves to be comforted by believing in Him.

If the child's death was accidental, they may think it all the more reason to turn away from God. Why wasn't he watching out for their daughter while she drove or swam? Why wasn't God in Germany, Korea, or Vietnam?

There are, of course, no soul-satisfying answers to these questions for the bereaved parent. He is stuck with deciding whether he believes or not, and no one can make that decision for him.

There is the story of the mother who chastised her son for not going to church willingly. "You go to the show for entertainment. You visit with your friends and have fun. Don't you think it is only right that you go to the Lord's house once a week for an hour?"

The boy thought about it and said, "But Mom, what would you think if you were invited to somebody's house and every time you went, the guy was never there?"

There are adults—bereaved parents—who believe the same thing. For these, coping with grief is frequently all the more difficult.

The poet James Russell Lowell wrote a poem nearly a hundred years ago, after his daughter Rose died, in which he illustrated the thinking process of a bereaved parent who turned away from religion. It is called "After the Burial":

Yes, faith is a goodly anchor;
When skies are sweet as a psalm,
At the bows it lolls so stalwart,
In its bluff, broad-shouldered calm.

And when over breakers to leeward
The tattered surges are hurled,
It may keep our head to the tempest,
With its grip on the base of the world.

But, after the shipwreck, tell me
What help in its iron thews,
Still true to the broken hawser,
Deep down among sea-weed and ooze?

In the breaking gulfs of sorrow,
When the helpless feet stretch out
And find in the deeps of darkness
No footing so solid as doubt,

Then better one spar of Memory
One broken plank of the Past,
That our human heart may cling to,
Though hopeless of shore at last!

To the spirit its splendid conjectures,
To the flesh its sweet despair,
Its tears o'er the thin-worn locket
With its anguish of deathless hair!

Immortal? I feel it and know it,
Who doubts it of such as she?
But that is the pang's very secret,—
Immortal away from me.

There's a narrow ridge in the graveyard
Would scarce stay a child in his race,
But to me and my thought it is wider
Than the star-sown vague of Space.

Your logic, my friend, is perfect,
Your moral most drearily true;
But, since the earth clashed on her coffin,
I keep hearing that, and not you.

Console if you will, I can bear it;
'Tis a well-meant alms of breath;
But not all the preaching since Adam
Has made Death other than Death.

It is pagan; but wait till you feel it,—
That jar of our earth, that dull shock
When the ploughshare of deeper passion
Tears down to our primitive rock.

Communion in spirit! Forgive me,
But I, who am earthly and weak,
Would give all my incomes from dreamland
For a touch of her hand on my cheek.

That little shoe in the corner,
So worn and wrinkled and brown,
With its emptiness confutes you,
And argues your wisdom down.

Lowell, not surprisingly, noted that the poem "has aroused strange echoes in men who assured me they were generally insensible to poetry."

Perhaps the reason for the strange echoes lies in his having voiced thoughts that are generally unspoken because they are uncomfortable for the nonbereaved to hear. "Forgive me, but I who am earthly and weak, would give all my incomes from dreamland for a touch of her hand on my cheek." I doubt very much that this thought hasn't crossed all our minds at least once when we have suffered through burying a child.

Recently, in speaking on religion in general, a friend who does not regularly go to church summed up his view of God and man's belief. What he said made a lot of sense and perhaps will be of some help to those who are angry at God because their child is dead.

He said, "The trouble with people is they view God in too personal a manner. They think of him as sitting and waiting to hear from them. That's ridiculous. He couldn't possibly hear each of us. What we have to do is think of God as the force who created this world and controls its overall destiny. I don't believe God hears individual prayers."

My friend's philosophy makes a lot of sense to me. Having personally gone from being deeply religious to almost nonreligious, and now landing somewhere in the middle, this conclusion suits me. It is comfortable for me.

Stephen Crane in *War is Kind* phrased this view succinctly when he explained the working of the world by saying: "A man said to the universe: 'Sir, I exist!' 'However,' replied the universe, 'the fact has not created in me a sense of obligation.' "

Crane was saying in effect what my friend had said.

My period of intense religiousness, although not by design, helped me through the first year of Robby's death in a very practical manner.

In the Jewish faith there is a prayer known as the Kaddish, in which the worshipper extolls God. Jews who have lost a dear one attend religious services daily, or whenever they wish, and recite the special mourner's Kaddish in memory of their dead. Among traditional Jews, only a Jewish male recites the mourner's Kaddish, but somehow, and to this day I do not know why, I felt a great need to break tradition and go to the Temple daily and take part in this service. In short order, it became a firm discipline.

I knew every day I would have to go to a prescribed place and utter certain words that were both a prayer for my dead son and a pleading for my own salvation. They were painful days, especially at first. But after a while, I began to develop a routine, to plan my day around the evening Kaddish service. Sometimes my children accompanied me. Sometimes I went with my husband. Often I went alone.

Today, I have come to the realization that the daily ritual was indeed a large part of my salvation. The disciplined routine made me face a dreadful truth daily and made me ultimately accept my loss. I believe my systematic routine brought me through my grieving perhaps a little sooner and a little more gently than others have been pulled through their grief.

The advantage of religious belief when a child dies is enormous. It is a source of comfort and, for those who choose to listen, it can answer the dread "Why?" But, realistically, a large part of our society is not religious. They believe neither in God nor in any organized praying. Yet, when they suffer bereavement, there can be some method such as the one I found to help ease the pain. If your faith offers no daily religious service, or if you do not choose to partake in one, set aside ten minutes a day, at the same time every day. Find a certain chair in a certain room and go to the same place daily. Take such a work as the "Prayer of Serenity" and say it daily and think about it as you repeat it.

> God grant me the serenity
> to accept the things I cannot change,
> courage to change the things I can,
> and the wisdom to know the difference.

For those who do not believe in God, change the first line to "I need the serenity."

Many poets have taken the theme of death and added new insights. Find poetry for your ten minutes of bereavement discipline. Look through it. You doubtless will discover some message that could be read daily.

John Greenleaf Whittier wrote a poem entitled "Forgiveness" which, upon careful examination, can be turned into a message for the bereaved parent who feels anger and hurt but does not pray. Reading it carefully, it cannot fail to remove some of the hostility against fortune we have all felt.

> *My heart was heavy, for its trust had been*
> *Abused, its kindness answered with foul wrong;*
> *So, turning gloomily from my fellow-men,*
> *One summer Sabbath day I strolled among*
> *The green mounds of the village burial place;*
> *Where, pondering how all human love and hate*
> *Find one sad level; and how, soon or late,*
> *Wronged and wrongdoer, each with meekened face,*
> *And cold hands folded over a still heart,*
> *Pass the green threshold of our common grave,*
> *Whither all footsteps tend, whence none depart,*
> *Awed for myself, and pitying my race,*
> *Our common sorrow, like a mighty wave,*
> *Swept all my pride away, and trembling I forgave!*

Use your ten minutes to think deeply whether with poetry or solitude. Use the time perhaps to think about your dead child but force yourself not to turn the sessions into ten minutes of hysteria. And when the time is up, above all, force yourself up from the chair and into some *activity*. It must be something where physical energy is used and not some passive endeavour such as watching television. Perhaps pick your ten minutes at the time which is busiest for you and therefore when you must get up at the end of the period and move about. In that way, you are assured of the success of this ten-minute period of introspection.

People who do not believe in a Supreme Being have often been defined as those who have no invisible means of support.

And almost nowhere can their additional burden be sensed more than when they lose a child.

They are left not only with the emptiness of their bereavement, they also must bear the weight of feeling there is no divine plan. This tragedy befell them with no vestige of hope even in another life.

One father, who said he is a second-generation atheist, explained his feelings when his daughter died.

"I look with envy upon those of you who believe. My intellect does not give me this freedom. Since Betty died I have learned there is little to comfort me in this life. For a nonbeliever faced with the death of his child there are not too many places to turn.

"There is not another Superman down the street to offer hope."

The father turned to my husband and me and asked just what hope our religion gives us, what it promises.

Being nonevangelistic—as is my husband—I tried to choose my answer carefully.

"The hope my faith gives me is that Robby did not die some stupid, meaningless, pointless death. That there was indeed a plan. A reason."

The atheist was scornful.

We found ourselves at a stalemate. I asked him what steps he was taking to help him through his grief.

"I think things through a great deal about my daughter and

her illness. Also, my mainstay is attending meetings where other parents have lost children from the same disease.

"Whenever the talk turns to religion I just shut up. But I will tell you, if there is a God, He must be very sadistic to want people to bow down and worship him while He whips you!"

As a believer, I find these sentiments uncomfortable. Yet, in writing a book of this kind, I cannot ignore nor make light of his view. I have met too many bereaved parents who feel as he does.

One woman who prides herself on having begun to function without any belief in God said, "I remember my child. But when a person feels survival depends solely upon herself she must think things through. It is not so much a matter of what happens as how you handle what happens.

"I go to the cemetery about six times a year. Not because I believe my child's spirit is hovering near but because this was the final place I ever saw her. I go there and reflect and cry. Sad as it may seem, I find this therapeutic."

Some nonbelieving parents have joined organizations whose members are bereaved persons and whose programmes examine bereavement. Of all things, they seem to derive the most benefit from meetings held on a regular basis. Some nonbelievers maintain that such organizations cannot be praised highly enough.

One man, in fact, made a rather interesting observation. "People generally become very defensive when I tell them I do not believe there is a God. But the oddest thing is that I meet with less hostility over my lack of believing at such meetings than in any other kind of situation.

"I guess because we are all feeling our way together we are forced to be more open-minded and receptive to different ideas.

"In all fairness, I don't ridicule people who do believe at these meetings as readily as I do in other places."

His view, of course, was entirely different from that of the father who simply clams up when religion is the issue. Yet, by meeting with other bereaved parents, each is given the opportunity to vent feelings and perhaps secure new and positive insights.

Obviously, the weight of coping, for a nonbeliever, is heaviest of all.

Where those who believe can reconcile themselves to the idea that someday they will know why their child died, a nonbeliever must rely solely on himself or herself to make some meaning out of the tragedy.

While religious people know ultimately they will be reunited with their son or daughter, atheists must accept that what they had with their child is all that will ever be except for their memories.

While believers have established places to pray for help and time-honoured guidelines to follow, an atheist must resort to his or her inner strength, solely.

In effect, a nonbeliever's burden rests heavily with himself or herself. It takes great strength, great fortitude to "go it alone."

But, the important thing about this sort of "going it alone" is that it must be limited to a lack of belief and not a lack of supportive people.

A friend, a counsellor, an organization of people caught up in the same catastrophe, are avenues that all nonbelievers should pursue.

As in all other stages of grieving, people are the most important ally to the bereaved parent.

Even for those who believe deeply in God, friends to talk with, to cry to, can be of great value.

*With the fearful strain that is on me
night and day, if I did not laugh I
should die.*

—ABRAHAM LINCOLN

BEREAVEMENT
AND
PLEASURE

Bereaved parents often find themselves in the oblique position of not appreciating what they are seeing because of the dun-coloured cloud that overshadows and changes the perspective of every place and every thing upon which they cast an eye.

All too often their senses are dulled and they fail to recognize what can still be marvellous or beautiful or just plain fun.

Worse, frequently, they do not understand the importance of being able to do so.

One of the major obstacles, in fact, to returning to the ordinary world of the living is this inability to accept pleasure. It is almost a feeling of "how could I laugh" or "how will I ever laugh again now that my child is dead." Yet, enjoyment is, after all, one of the most important survival tools we possess. It

121

is one of the things we can do in our fight to endure after the loss of a child.

We took our first big plunge back into the world of enjoyment with a weekend trip to Las Vegas four months after Robby died.

I remember sitting in a nightclub listening to the uproariously funny routine of a well-known comedian and laughing until my sides ached. The laughter and its intensity felt almost cleansing.

Certainly, I paid for my pleasure later that evening because, once we returned to our hotel room, I cried as violently as I had laughed just hours earlier.

But the important thing, then, was that a step had been taken, a beginning made.

There were times after that Las Vegas trip when I was afraid to go out and have fun. I remembered the intensity of my anguish back in that hotel room, and it would seem not worth the effort just for a little enjoyment. After all, my price for pleasure was intense pain.

This sense of anguish lacks gender. My husband felt exactly as I did. Yet we bolstered each other and still "enjoyed" a social life.

Looking back now, I realize that every time I put myself on the line and chanced pleasure, it strengthened me and made me able ultimately to enjoy much of life. Certainly, I am able to enjoy more than I ever dreamt possible after Robby died.

Many people whose children have died say their experiences were similar. Whether the first trip out was to a movie, a restaurant, or a card game, the initial reentering into society was frightening.

Men, usually the family providers, are not given the choice about leaving home. Some claim that the step of seeking entertainment is not so great for them as for their wives, who have been able to hide out at home.

One husband who fitted this pattern saw his wife was sinking deeper into her grief while he, because of his job, was forced to cope—at least on a surface level.

Three months after his daughter died, he decided to take his wife to a lovely restaurant, hoping to help her escape the miasma of gloom in their home. The evening was a fiasco because his wife sat in an elegant dining room and wept.

Despite the failure of the dinner itself, the man said he knew even as they sat in the restaurant that a victory of sorts had been achieved.

"Once we had gone that far, I knew something had been gained," he said. "Even though Barbara cried and I could barely down my dinner, there was no doubt that we had won a victory. I knew it would take a little less courage to go to dinner the second time and the third time. Months and years have proven I was correct."

Vacations, especially family vacations, are another thing to be faced and dealt with after a child dies. At first you will be certain that you cannot go and have a good time. If you do decide to go for the sake of the children or just because you desperately need a change of pace, it is important to know you will face an inevitable letdown when you return home.

We have been tent campers for many years. Robby was just an infant the first time we went. He loved it. After he died, we were certain that never again could we go and enjoy being in the woods, relaxing. Our children insisted, however, that they wanted to continue camping because it was our family hobby. Robby was not the only one who enjoyed it. We finally agreed, that first summer after he died, to give it a try. We were sad at first, but in a matter of days found ourselves once again getting into the spirit of things. Our walks in the woods together, and swimming, and the bonfire with hot dogs and roasted marshmallows forged a bond with our surviving children that has remained strong through these intervening years. It was a good trip.

What we were not prepared for was the sudden rush of sadness that overcame us when we returned home. We wished we had been warned because our reaction was startling in its intensity. I remember turning to my husband, tears running down my cheeks, and saying, "He is still dead. He will always be dead."

Perhaps knowing we would experience this emotion upon returning home would have lessened its impact. There is still to this day a residue, although slight, of the pain in returning home after being away on vacation.

But we carry our sadness. It does not carry us. It does not prevent us from living as rounded a life as we possibly can build.

Dr. Joseph Fischoff, chief of psychiatry of Children's Hospital of Michigan, said learning to enjoy life once again is essential to the healing process when a child dies.

"It is important to understand you are not abandoning a dead child by laughing. It's all right to enjoy life. That does not mean you have forgotten your dead son or daughter. This is a very difficult truth for bereaved parents to accept."

Because the loss has been tremendous, sometimes bereaved parents swing too far the other way. Pleasure, pleasure, regardless of costs, can in the long run prove harmful. As a tribute to life, many parents will overspend on weddings and other happy occasions for living children.

One mother put it succinctly when she said, "I know I should not have gone whole hog for my daughter's wedding. But we have a dead son. It costs so much to take care of a child in a terminal illness, we felt what a joy it would be to spend money on a happy thing like a beautiful wedding for our daughter, who is alive."

Parents who are fortunate enough never to have undergone the death of a child can sometimes not understand this need to do things lavishly for living children.

Having done much the same for our son when he reached his thirteenth birthday and we celebrated his Bar Mitzvah, a Jewish religious custom marking a boy's entrance into the ranks of manhood, I recall feeling thankful, so thankful, that we had a child for whom to give this beautiful party. It was lavish, extravagant, and soul satisfying. It served, I think, as a testimonial to life, at least for us.

As our son stood before the congregation momentarily my thoughts were with Robby, who had died seven months earlier. We would never see him stand there and read from ancient Hebrew text. Never would my husband stand, as Jewish fathers have always stood, with Robby as he read from the scroll and recited blessings thousands of years old.

This thought, I have discovered, creeps in during all happy occasions. I am left with a pang which is, thankfully, momentary. As on that Friday evening when our son was Bar Mitzvah and my thoughts left Robby and went to our present splendid young man, I felt a deep gratitude. I doubt whether parents who have never undergone the death of a child could understand our jubilation. We felt a sense of continuity and above all a sense that not everything had been lost and buried.

Most bereaved parents experience this feeling. Whether it is the confirmation or baptism or sweet sixteen of a surviving child, we feel a momentary sorrow and sense of loss and then a gratitude that we are still left with something that gives us pleasure or elation or contentment.

In experiencing this, however, a word of caution must be introduced. Although we are elated, there comes a time to put the brakes on, financially. Some couples come near financial ruin because their need to make up to themselves for their pain is enormous. Though the need is understandable, it is dangerous. As in all things, when one approaches matters maturely, there must be a middle-of-the-road method of enjoying oneself.

Cars, clothes, parties, fancy restaurants, all can help to heal. But it is foolish to try to overcome a child's death by plunging into a spending spree that can be backbreaking.

It is wrong to sink everything we possess into pleasure, and this is a mistake many bereaved parents make. It is equally wrong never to take the chance, never to spend the money on enjoyment. You need time out more than most people.

Bereaved parents generally go through a period akin to living in hell. Laughing is wrong, pleasure is wrong. That they have survived is wrong. Actually, we often feel nothing positive exists any longer for us. But living in hell is something that need not be.

There is an old story about two senators who became angry and one told the other to "go to hell." The senator who had been told to depart on this long hot journey went to the governor and asked him to do something about it.

The governor, a wily and sage man, walked to the library in his study and took down a law volume. After leafing through a number of pages, he solemnly turned to the aggrieved senator and said, "I have looked up the law as you have seen and you don't have to go!"

Neither do bereaved parents have to go, despite our having felt, through the dark days of our loss, that hell had come to us.

Perhaps the key to dealing with pleasure lies in acquiring the secure inner knowledge that you are not abandoning your dead child nor are you abandoning your grieving even though you go out on Saturday night or have people in for cards or dinner.

This fear of abandoning death is most common to bereaved parents, and because of it we feel a needless guilt when trying to put the pieces of our lives back together again. I remember the two thoughts that pounded away at me in the Las Vegas hotel room. First, how could I laugh? In the fantasies and misconceptions about bereavement, I felt like an unnatural mother, a heartless, unfeeling person who could consider having fun with her child newly dead. This is, of course, nonsense. The only way to survive bereavement is to step away from it occasionally!

Second—and this I have come to understand is the crux of the problem of dealing with pleasure—I kept feeling that by laughing I had left Robby alone "out there." It was as if my grief served as an umbilical cord to keep him close to me. A part of me. My laughter brought about a sense of "letting go" and I was by no means ready to let go of him. My sorrow, in effect, kept Robby and me wrapped together and I still wanted that badly.

When I came squarely to terms with why I thought laughing and pleasure equalled betrayal rather than survival, I allowed logic to intrude upon my grief. Robby was no farther away nor any closer to me regardless of my emotional state. I was not betraying him. I was not abandoning him. I was not leaving him alone when I laughed. I could not hold him closer when I cried. He was dead despite what I did or did not do.

With this reasoned out, I began accepting social invitations, and in spite of some rather difficult times in the privacy of our home before going out and after returning, slowly, very slowly, one successful outing built upon another. I would remind myself before going out that this did not mean I no longer grieved for my child. Such a reminder helped ease my mind. It may help ease yours and free you once again to live and take pleasure in living.

In the world's broad field of battle, in the bivouac of Life, be not like dumb, driven cattle! Be a hero in the Strife!

—HENRY WADSWORTH LONGFELLOW

BEREAVEMENT AND FUNCTIONING

Once in the days of ancient Greece, a man who was lame volunteered to serve in the army.

He walked, limping, toward the commanding general's tent where he sought to be inducted into an elite battle corps. Observing his lameness, a group of soldiers began to jeer.

The man won the day, the respect of the general, and a place in the army unit when he turned to his tormentors and replied, "I am here to fight, not to run!"

Indeed, the man had something that could well serve as a guide for those of us who have dead children and are seeking to return to the world of the living. Yes, reentering that world is a battle, one that is all the more difficult because we are entering it battered and limping. But that does not mean we cannot make it. We just have to understand it will not be easy.

One mother, whose son died when the roof of an abandoned building collapsed on him, said that each time she accepts a tennis invitation is as hard as the first time. But because she has a genuine desire to cope not only for herself but for her family she still accepts those invitations.

"Tennis was an important part of my life before the accident. Each time I go it's like proving to myself that sometime the pain will ease up. One day I really will be able to go about my life without its taking such effort. Such energy."

There was a period after Robby died when I floated and just went through the mechanical motions of cooking and cleaning and holding banal conversations. It was a time of numbness. Conversely, it was a time when the pain was so intense it was actually physical. I recall feeling I had undergone the amputation of a leg or arm.

It was then I experienced my greatest fear as a survivor. Horrified and frozen, I used to think "What if it would always be like this? What if the pain never stopped?" The thought of endless days spent in a quicksand of grief pulling me farther and farther down from any semblance of normalcy frequently panicked me.

Eventually though, after a few months, both the panic and physical pain subsided and I felt reassured I would survive. It was only then I decided I actually wanted to.

Functioning even at the simplest level is not easy after a child dies. In fact, it is a very frightening time. Suddenly, everyday things begin to loom large because your senses actually feel distorted.

I recall the first day we left our house following the week-long period of mourning we observed. I was almost affronted that cars still drove up and down streets and businesses still operated. I felt vulnerable.

One mother said it was a shock when she realized garbage

men were still picking up refuse even though her son was dead.

Because they have been stopped short, bereaved parents come to feel the whole world has come to a standstill during that initial period just after the child's death. It is shocking to discover this is not at all the case. The world has gone on. Life has gone on.

For the bereaved parent, functioning is somewhat like jumping aboard an already moving bus. You are out of breath, somewhat dishevelled, but in motion nonetheless.

The first rule in trying to function is not to bite off more than you can chew. Start small. Begin with essential everyday tasks. Work, cook, shop, pay your bills. Those things must be done. Make sure you complete your projects. It is very easy to become distracted when grieving. Then, gradually, add a few chores that can be—and have been—put off. Balance your chequebook, file all those office letters you have let pile up, clean out that ridiculously overstuffed cupboard.

When you are comfortable at that level, take the next step and slowly begin to avail yourself of life's small niceties. Apply a new eye shadow, change a hairstyle, or set the dinner table with flowers. For a man, simple things like bringing home a bottle of wine to share at dinner, buying a frivolous golf hat or sport shirt, or painting the front door are easy to accomplish.

Decide on a particular "treat" the day before. When the new day comes, make certain you follow through even though you cry as you go to the store for that something new. Insist to yourself you *must* do this thing. Repeat this formula enough times and you will come to realize that doing some little thing above and beyond the business of actual existence is the beginning of living.

It may come as a surprise that once you have taken the first step, others follow. Of course, there will be times you falter and seem to go backward. But, as time goes on, the setbacks become smaller and fewer while the momentum of living propels you forward.

Remember, this does not all come about overnight. You will not awaken one morning miraculously filled with a joy of life. You will not leave your sadness behind; to be told you could is neither realistic nor truthful. But, instead, your sadness will no longer pull you down. You will now carry it with you, inside you. Remember this: you will carry it. It will not carry you!

Another step that is essential is to regroup and strengthen the remaining family unit—and this is critical. It is not enough to all be at home and acting like the living dead. Nor is it enough to take the other way out by constantly running and rarely remaining at home with your memories.

Memories have a way of catching up with you anyhow. As in many other avenues of life, there is a middle ground between sitting home always and never being there. Reaching that point and achieving that balance—and how much of each is an individual family thing—is very important. Try different at-home and away patterns. Experiment until you find the combination that is right for you.

Devote at least a small portion of every evening to your children, their schoolwork, their problems. Do the same for your mate. Don't begin with long doses of either, because if you do you will feel the frustration of knowing your attention span is minimal. Gradually, you will discover an increase in that attention span and in the amount of time during which you can give active attention to your family.

A very difficult area of functioning is coming to grips with the knowledge that there is absolutely no way of getting around holidays and vacations. Celebrations, Christmas and birthdays will come despite your best efforts to avoid them. And they are horrendous times for many years. Their pain cannot be minimized. But they still must be faced.

One family, trying to avoid Thanksgiving—which was the

dead child's birthday as well—decided that family gatherings were no longer for them. They would travel or simply ignore the festivities.

One day the mother came upon her ten-year-old daughter crying and asked what was wrong.

"She was sobbing," reported the mother. "All the children in school had told of their plans and made table decorations for the holiday and Lynn felt completely removed from her classmates. She cried that she was not only deprived of her brother who was dead, but she couldn't even have Thanksgiving dinner and a turkey!

"I listened to her and held her in my arms and cried. What she was saying made sense. After all, we still had three living children. They also mattered. That night I talked to my husband and we decided that, no matter how bleak and empty it would be, we would have a traditional Thanksgiving dinner."

The mother said the family sat around the table, very quietly at first. The father said grace and thanked the Lord for a bountiful meal. When he was through, their ten-year-old said she had something to add.

"I want to thank Mommy and Daddy for making this very special dinner for our family. And most of all I want to thank you God for having let us have my brother Eric for six years."

The mother who will never forget what her daughter said told me there was not a dry eye at the table for a few minutes. But gradually, as the meal progressed, they made an effort to discuss why the holiday was celebrated. From there, the parents told of amusing experiences at Thanksgiving dinners in their younger years. The mother said she planned to tell the stories to lighten the atmosphere just as carefully as she planned her menu. By the time the meal was over, the parents discovered what had been built up in their minds as unsurvivable had become just another turning point.

There will be many such turning points as you work your

way forward. You have already survived what you were certain you could not live through—the death of your child. Turning points, plateaux, are merely steps in coping and nothing more. As you go through each holiday, each season, each happy-sad occasion, you will gain strength from having passed beyond yet another painful event.

Though resuming daily routines is vital, some psychiatric personnel believe that a drastic change in certain areas can be of great benefit not only to an individual but to a married couple. One psychologist who often counsels bereaved parents claims a prime method of keeping the marriage intact is change, change, and more change.

"Since your family has undergone this indefensible event, it is ridiculous to pretend there was no impact and that things will go on as before. That is why change is so critical," he said.

"Alter the seating arrangement at the dinner table, for instance. There can be no benefit to eating your meals looking at the empty spot your dead child once occupied."

Using the word "recreativity," he counsels couples to take up hobbies together because that will strengthen the marriage. That something, he insists, must be innovative, something they had never done before as a unit.

One professional couple is taking up upholstery. Another couple is involved in extensive travel, a novelty to this pair who rarely left the city.

Important as a unit project is, there appears to be a great need to create something individually after a child dies.

Members of a group of bereaved parents who call themselves "First Sunday" have discussed their personal methods of functioning. In general, most men and women, even those who have done nothing of the sort before, turn to some creative endeavour to help ease their grief. Whether it is in art or a project such as carpentry, bereaved parents seem to feel a need to make something, to bring something to life.

Although I have been writing as far back in my life as I can remember, I never sought this outlet as a career until after Robby died. Then my need to "do something" was nearly insatiable.

It was at that time I discovered another truth about functioning when a child dies. I was no longer afraid to attempt things.

I still remember the first time I brought a proposed article to our local weekly newspaper. I was frightened until I stopped to think there was nothing to lose. After all, I had survived the death of my son. Facing an unknown editor was really nothing beside that. It is this thought that has given me a sense of poise in the years since Robby died.

In coping with life's problems, there is very little that should be able to frighten a bereaved parent when it comes to functioning or achieving as a business person, social service volunteer, artist, or whatever holds your interest. You may even want to take a stab at returning to school. Remember, we are different from other people. For most of us, the worst is behind us. It is not something we still have to face.

To my own satisfaction I have now defined fear. Fear is waiting for a doctor to tell you whether your child will live or die! That is a truth that all bereaved parents can profit from if they learn it and learn it well.

It was not long after my stint at the weekly paper that I took a deep breath and applied for a job on a major newspaper. I was accepted on a part-time basis and my elation was almost boundless. I could achieve. I could accomplish. I could *do*!

One psychologist said that as important as he believes re-creativity to be, it is equally urgent not to make changes in some areas. It is important, for instance, to stay local and not make quick decisions about moving out of town. After all, in most cases, your supportive people are where you now live.

He said it is also important to "confront" holidays—but to rearrange the table and the previous order in which things were done.

One family, instead of opening Christmas presents in the morning, now opens them the night before, as an example. And in our home we now have a Hannukah party that includes all the cousins instead of merely limiting it to our immediate family.

Probably more when a child dies than in any other situation, a positive example of people functioning can have great impact.

Frequently organizations where bereaved parents come to air their grief and listen to methods others have employed in coping can have immeasurable value.

One woman, an older widow, attended such a meeting. She gravitated to another woman, a laughing woman who during the coffee hour regaled those around her with a tale of being surveyed about a new brand of bandage. She told how she had promised to wear the new product for three days and nights. She said her neighbors roared when they saw her knees with one bandage clearly marked "Brand X" and the other "Brand Y."

The widow observed with amazement this woman who was about the same age as herself. She, too, had been approached for this survey and had refused to take part "because her heart wasn't in it."

The other woman explained that she forced herself to participate in things, and wouldn't it be a good idea for everyone?

The widow nodded. She saw the contrast between herself and the other woman. Both were older. Both had dead children, yet one of them laughed and took part in some of life's silliness.

It was evident to everyone in the little group that a new approach had been introduced to the widow.

There are also parents who pick up the pieces by commemorative works. One Western family established a scholarship fund so other youngsters could receive a college education even though their own daughter never lived to graduate. Another family, very wealthy, donated a major gymnasium in memory of their boy who died young. One family established a hospital memorial fund. Still another plans to build a zoo in the South in memory of their dead son. Television personality Art Linkletter, whose daughter committed suicide while apparently under the influence of an hallucinogenic drug, is actively supporting legislation to liberalize California's marijuana penalties. He has campaigned for drug abuse education since 1969 when his daughter Diane, twenty, jumped to her death.

These people, on their own social and economic planes, felt the need to undertake some project of importance to offset even in a small way the tragedy of their children's deaths. There are many parents of lesser means who commemorate their dead children. What seems to be universal among all of us who have dead children is a need to do something meaningful with our energies.

One method some bereaved parents have found helpful, especially those with little money, is to become involved with children who are motherless and fatherless. While I would never suggest adopting a child with the hope of replacing a dead son or daughter, certainly the idea of befriending such a youngster and visiting with him makes a lot of sense. No one can replace your child that died. I believe no one should seek replacements because every human being, regardless of age—and this means the young babies who die of cot death too—is his own unique personality and no one can become somebody else.

But, by visiting orphanages and homes for retarded children, bereaved parents can bring a measure of comfort to lonely youngsters and, by doing so, some of their own loneliness is lessened, their perspective lengthened.

There are still other parents who, instead of donating memorials to their dead children, live as such memorials.

One woman, whose son died at the age of five of leukemia, makes it a point to write letters to people she hears about whose children have died recently. Her notes are not sloppy and tearful. Instead, they are intended to tell parents that they will survive the tragedy. She did. She has been thanked long afterward by people with whom she corresponded.

On a larger scale, and one that requires more energy, is the example of Mrs. Sylvia Brown, executive director of the Children's Leukemia Foundation of Michigan. Nearly twenty-three years ago, Mrs. Brown noticed that her two-year-old child had developed a number of black and blue marks on her legs. She could think of no reason for them because the child did not fall that often. Somewhat alarmed, she called her child's paediatrician who asked that the youngster be taken to the hospital for examination.

Blood tests confirmed what her doctor already suspected. Little Sandra Ann was the victim of leukaemia. Within a month she was dead.

Mrs. Brown vividly remembers the time immediately after.

"I would sit there, wearing dark clothes, and think over and over again, "Why me, God? Why me?" This went on for several weeks until one day my five-year-old daughter came up to me and asked if I was still her mommy.

"She startled me and I asked what she meant. Abby said I couldn't be her mommy because her mommy never wore ugly black clothes like I was wearing and her mommy used to be happy and not always sad.

"It was then I realized I still had a husband and another child to live for. I forced myself out of my depression and began taking an interest in things again."

Among the interests Mrs. Brown developed was that of visiting young leukaemia victims in hospitals and befriending their parents.

About six years later, Mrs. Brown received a phone call from a woman who wanted to start a leukaemia foundation and was trying to gather people who had children sick and dying of the disease.

"Her phone call struck a responsive chord. I felt the need to help people. When I needed it, no one was there. I had felt as if my husband and I were the only ones in the world who had had this dreadful thing happen."

Mrs. Brown said the phone call also unleashed anger at herself.

"How could I have let something like this happen to my daughter and not have done something about it for other children, other parents?

"I began to try and resolve how we could help others cope with leukaemia. I work very hard, but I still get a lot more out of the organization than I put into it. Advances are being made. I live for the day when there will be a cure for leukaemia. Then I know my work will be done."

Mrs. Brown is perhaps more fortunate than many bereaved parents. She at least has determined what direction will most benefit not only herself but others. As in most difficult things in life, we each must find our own way at our own level in order to function in a positive manner.

When I began to accept the premise that functioning despite my sadness was like hiking with a heavy backpack that could not be removed, I underwent a marked change in attitude. I decided I wanted to cope, to function, to walk through the forest, even though I was burdened with a great weight.

Mere survival, mere existence, is no longer enough for me and should not be for you.

Anyone can exist. But you have endured more pain than just anyone. You have undergone the ultimate tragedy. You owe yourself more than a shuffling-along existence. You owe yourself some surefooted living.

The happiest parent is the one who knows what to remember in the past, what to enjoy in the present, and what to plan in the future.

—ANONYMOUS

BEREAVEMENT AND THE REST OF YOUR LIFE

There is an old story about two blind men trying to earn their rather sad living by selling pencils on a busy New York corner.

An observer, feeling pity, watched the two men who stood separated by a few feet. As he looked on, he noticed that most people bypassed one blind man but stopped short in front of the other. Few failed to buy from him.

Curious, the observer stepped closer and learned the reason for the obvious disparity of how passersby responded to the two. The first blind man, on his cup, had a sign which read: "Please help the blind."

The second, the successful man, too had a sign. But his read: "It is spring and I am blind."

The same affliction, the same need for revenue, but a different approach.

We bereaved parents are much like the two blind men. We are faced with a dreadful situation. What we must now do is determine how best to handle the tragedy and achieve what we want—a way to live with it—and most of that handling lies in the approach.

When a child dies, at first surviving is like an affliction. Indeed, it bears some similarity to blindness because we are left without seeing a path we can safely follow to soothe our torn senses. We must grope our way forward. Stumbling, picking ourselves up again until we learn how to handle our grief, is about all we can do.

If intellect is employed in dealing with that grief, there is a way out of bereavement that can leave the parent whole and sighted and a survivor in a positive rather than a negative sense.

Just after Robby died, the idea of living for any appreciable length of time was horrifying. All I could envision was an endless number of hours and days stretching into infinity and all filled with pain and grief.

No one who had not undergone the experience of having a child die could have convinced me this would not be the case. I simply would not have believed him.

Now I find myself and my family going and doing and functioning and taking a joy in life and its challenges. I never believed this would be possible. But I assure you it is true.

Long before Robby died, I would lie awake and visualize him dead. I would walk the halls and sit in the living room most nights fearful about what life would be like should he not survive his heart surgery. Only the worst, most dreadful pictures came to mind. In the year from the time we scheduled his surgery until he died, I do not believe I slept more than three hours any night. The rest of the time I would spend seeing him dead and seeing our lives as an ongoing time of sorrow.

Never did I envision us laughing and happy and dealing with life. I would not have thought it possible to rise above the tragedy, but we did and so can you.

You probably never thought you could live through your child's funeral. What could have been more dreadful? But you did.

Certainly surviving all the grief you felt seemed impossible. Those days and nights of crying, exhaustion, and pain were almost beyond endurance. You were certain, at times, you would never get past that time in your life. But you did.

There were times you felt great guilt because somehow you had not filled the role of "parent" as society interprets the role. You were unable to save your child and keep it alive. As that cold, clammy feeling would come over you and your back would prickle thinking about what you could have done differently, you were sunk into such a pit of grieving that you never dreamed it would be possible to go on. But you did.

Often, you were beset with anger and a feeling of powerlessness because events that should have been in your control simply were not. You did not think you could overcome these feelings—especially the hopelessness that accompanied them. But you can.

Just when you needed your mate most, you would find he or she could help you least. You expected comfort from someone incapable of comforting. You argued. Sometimes you even hated. You never thought you would rise from the bottom of the well of sorrow. But you can.

You thought never again could you take an interest in the world and retain friendships and attend weddings and happy occasions for other people's children. You were certain you could never live through the trauma. But you will.

There was no doubt in your mind that you never again could enjoy yourself. Never want to travel. Never give parties—or attend them. Never have fun. You would only be sorrowful and certainly you would never laugh. Above all, not laugh. But you will.

And most of all, you were sure it would be impossible for you to function as a whole human being not buffeted by the waves of sorrow that swept over you in the early days of your tragedy. But you will.

You will do all that and you will do more.

Everything you have achieved—and just going about your day-to-day business after such a tragedy is an accomplishment —will act as a stepping stone to anything else you ever try to do.

The fear of the unknown is behind us, for most of us, because we have already taken a long look at hell.

Understand and accept that, for you, there is still a future and one that can be as bright and good as you choose to make it.

You have before you the rest of your life. What you do with it is entirely a matter of choice. There are no rules or laws that require you to mourn forever and you certainly should not.

One man, whose daughter died six months ago, said he always feels strange about accepting a golf date.

"What will people say if I go out on the course and become excited over a good shot? They will think there's something wrong with me for not showing my sorrow all the time."

That man expressed a fear that is common to most bereaved parents. What will people say? How will it look? We all, especially in the beginning of this long sojourn back from the valley of the shadow of death, are sensitive to how we appear to our friends and neighbours. We, most of us, want people to understand we are grieving regardless of what we are doing.

About a month after Robby died, the principal of his school announced that a special tree in Robby's memory would be planted on the front lawn of the school. Each student who wished to contribute was asked to bring a certain amount of money. No student was allowed to bring more because the principal wanted everyone to be a part of this enormous life experience—this memorial to a fellow student.

Naturally we were asked to attend the ceremony. On the day the Robby-tree was planted we arrived a bit early still badly rocked by our month-long grieving but yet capable of behaving civilly. Knowing that every student from the kindergarten to the sixth grade would be present, we would not have attended if we could not have handled the situation.

But we were able to handle it and even laugh at something humorous someone said before the little service began, with the lowered flag and "taps" and a young boy making a farewell speech to his dead friend.

It was then, when we laughed, that I became aware of a strange feeling that somehow I had done the wrong thing. I should not have laughed. I seem to recall a few rather surprised faces on some of the adults. For, shocked and horrified as they were feeling at that moment and overwhelmed with their own empathy, it must have appeared utterly unnatural for the dead boy's parents to be able to laugh.

It was then, as I said, that I became conscious of that paralytic "what will people think" mentality. Worrying about that kind of thinking is false and trivial. I believe it also can dangerously retard your reentry into society. If Person A believes you should wait to go out to dinner for six months and Person B believes you must not laugh for eight months and Person C thinks you should not have company for a year and you allow yourself to be buffeted by these outside judgments at the time of your supreme vulnerability you will not do what is right for *you* but what *other* people who have not been through your ordeal *think* is right for you.

I was lucky enough to understand what I was feeling and did not allow myself to be guided by someone else's timetable for what is acceptable. Instead, I let my inner instincts for self-preservation remain my determinant. We all have these instincts. Use yours. Listen to them. They can be excellent judgmental tools.

The truth is, few can undertand what we are feeling unless they too have been there!

In trying to live the rest of your life it is imperative not to make "what will the neighbours think" your prime consideration. Instead, concern yourself with functioning as best you can.

As long as I live I will be sorry Robby is dead. That is fact. That is something I carry always. There are times, especially the good times, when I miss him still. But there are still good times. We share joys as a family that he did not live to share and I am sorry. But we still have joys. That is as it should be for us. That is as it should be for you.

HELPFUL ORGANISATIONS

The Compassionate Friends, 53 North Street, Bristol BS3 1EN
  0845 120 3785
  www.tcf.org.uk
CRUSE Bereavement Care, PO Box 800, Richmond, Surrey
  TW9 1RG 0844 477 9400
  www.crusebereavementcare.org.uk